A L   P A R R

PUPPY CARE
The Pack Leader´s Way

Beginner's Guide to Raise Your New Puppy!

Basic Dog Training with Cesar Millan, Karl Lorenz and B. F. Skinner

GRAPEVINE BOOKS
2016

DISCLAIMER

Author: Al Parr

Published by: Grapevine Books/Ediciones De La Parra

Cesar Millan Cover Photo: *DodgersMomPhotography* (Wikimedia Commons)

https://commons.wikimedia.org/wiki/File:Cesar_millan_(cropped).jpg

Lorenz and Skinner Cover Photos: Wikimedia Commons (modified)

ISBN-13: 978-1539991731
ISBN-10: 1539991733

C O N T E N T

FOREWORD

ABOUT THIS BOOK

THERE REALLY IS NOTHING quite as adorable as a puppy!

Puppies hey are cute, cuddly and full of love to give! But if they are left untrained they can also be a real nuisance! Just ask me!

The problem with puppies that are not trained is that they are always getting in trouble and finally grow into untrained dogs. And an untrained dog, apart from generating trouble, can also be very dangerous and even become a threat to your community.

Truth is, there are many reasons for your puppy to be trained and learn to obey basic commands like "come", "stay", "no", and "sit", among others, which will not only help you control his behavior, but will also help you keep him out of trouble.

As the Mexican American dog trainer, best-selling author, public speaker and internationally acclaimed television host Cesar Millan points out, *"new puppy owners often make the mistake of endlessly worrying about finding the right puppy treats or bed. But they spend little or no time worrying about how or what they will teach their new puppy."*

This guidebook is based on my own analysis, research, and experience, as well as the basic teachings of Cesar Millan, Karl Lorenz and B. F. Skinner. Its pages will show what you need to train your new puppy the pack-leader's way: From setting up the training area and getting the equipment and supplies you will need, to claiming your role as pack leader and conditioning him to obey your basic commands.

ON BECOMING A PACK LEADER

Although becoming your puppy's pack leader is a relatively simple process, certain basic requirements must be met: From learning the basics of pack leadership, dog psychology and canine conditioning, to knowing how to use the reward system, repetition, and basic commands.

Finding the right puppy treats or bed is part of what you need to do and is also described in these pages. But as Cesar points out, your top priority at this point should definitely be becoming your puppy´s pack leader, a condition that will certainly help you connect with him. And having that connection will certainly make it easier to train your young dog:

> *"Yes, a puppy needs nutritious food and a safe, warm place to live. But another equally powerful and important biological necessity is the need for a strong pack leader to serve as the dominant source of alpha energy in their lives…*
>
> *"Puppies sense our confidence levels and will take control if they perceive us as weak. When dogs or puppies take control, bad behaviors, such as excessive barking, leash-pulling, or anxiety, will develop. Therefore, the most important thing you can do is to become your puppy's pack leader. And this means demonstrating leadership from day one. Remember,*

puppies don't crave a fancy treat or bed;
they need you to become their stable pack
leader to demonstrate love in a way they
understand."

All I can say is that if you really love your new puppy and expect to share a long and happy life with him, then you need to apply the basic principles of pack-leader training contained in this book, which will not only show you the basics of pack leadership and dog psychology, but also how to assume a leading role from day one!

LESSON ONE

YOU AND YOUR PUPPY

GETTING A NEW PUPPY is a fun and interesting event!

You probably went to a breeder or pet store, or maybe just saw an ad on the Internet or the newspaper for puppies, and decided just to check it out. Before you knew it those little eyes and fluffy puppy fur had your heart melting and you were headed home with him or her in your arms. If you are like most new pet owners you had visions of playing fetch with your puppy, of watching him frolic at the lake, and of cuddling up on cold nights.

However, you probably failed to realize that the behaviors you dream of in a dog do not come naturally.

In fact, "natural" behaviors for most puppies include lovely little things like chewing up your favorite shoes, barking every second of the day, and peeing wherever they are when the mood strikes them.

These behaviors might seem cute at first, or even manageable but, if left unchecked, they can lead to serious problems during adulthood.

Once you get your puppy, you should spend most of your time around the house with your new dog, making him feel comfortable and getting him on a puppy schedule.

If you can't be with your puppy, then plan to have someone else with him in the meantime.

You should not get a puppy the day before you leave on a two week vacation. The best time to get a puppy is Friday after work so you have at least two full days to spend solely on housebreaking.

WHY TRAIN YOUR PUPPY

Like I mentioned in the *Foreword*, the problem with puppies that are not trained is that they grow into untrained dogs.

And an untrained dog can be a real nuisance!

You will need to train your puppy in many ways. From teaching him where to defecate to obeying basic commands like "come", "stay", "no", and "sit", among others that will help you control his behavior and keep him out of trouble.

All dogs bite. It is in their nature to defend with everything they have, including their teeth. Therefore you have to teach your dog not to use their teeth so that no one winds up hurt, at least not when they are playing with them.

While we all expect our dog to protect us in a worst-case scenario situation, you should train your dog to be non-confrontational.

Also, all of that cute little yipping can quickly become loud barking that keeps you and your neighbors up for nights on end. And the little teeth marks in your shoes can turn into destroyed furniture and a destroyed home before you know it!

Likewise, those cute little puppy poops are not so cute when the dog is 75 pounds and has the excrement to match.

People grow tired of dogs that never grow up, and then they take those dogs to the shelter. We all know how sad life can be for a shelter dog and the end that many of those dogs meet.

Dogs that pose a danger to the community are at risk of being put down. In addition, those that are problematic for any of the reasons listed above often wind up homeless.

So if you really love your new puppy and intent to have a long and happy life with it, make sure to train him appropriately. And for best results, apply the principles contained in this book and train him the pack-leader´s way!

COGNITIVE DEVELOPMENT

Just like humans, dogs go through a series of cognitive development as they grow up. Puppies, like babies, learn to interact with the world around them at around eight weeks of age. They will also mimic behaviors early in life, so if you have one well behaved dog your puppy can learn from him. If this is your only canine do not worry, they will also learn by watching you.

Just like parenting, dog training is something that often happens while you are paying attention to other things. This is what is popularly known as "unconscious training". Puppies are constantly learning. So, those first few months that you have a puppy are an incredibly important time to really focus on training your dog.

It can be a lot of work but in the end both you and your dog will be much happier!

LESSON TWO

PACK LEADERSHIP

WHAT IS PRESENTLY KNOWN AS *"PACK LEADERSHIP"* originally derived from the works of the Austrian zoologist, animal behaviorist and founder of ethological research Konrad Lorenz, author of *"King Solomon's Ring"* (1949) and *"Man Meets Dog"* (1950).

Pack leadership was more recently developed by contemporary researchers and dog trainers, including Cesar Millan, who perfected it, giving it its present form.

The original version of pack leadership was based on Lorenz's view of the role of natural leaders in wolf packs, as he described in "*Man Meets Dog*":

> *"In order to obtain enough nourishment for its large requirements, the wolf pack is obliged to cover great distances, when the members must support each other staunchly in their attacks on big game. An exacting social organization, true loyalty to the pack-leader and the absolute mutual support of all its members are the conditions for success in the hard struggle for existence of this species.*

> *"These properties of the wolf explain without any doubt the very noticeable difference in disposition between jackal and Lupus dogs, while is quite apparent to people with a real understanding of dogs. While the former treat their masters as parent animals, the latter see them more in the light of pack-leaders and their behavior towards them is correspondingly different."*

Regarding what he called "*the dependence of a dog on his*

master", Lorenz stated in his book:

> *"The dependence of a dog on his master has two quite distinct origins; it is largely due to a lifelong maintenance of those ties which bind the young wild dog to its mother, but which in the domestic dog remain part of a lifelong preservation of youthful characters. The other root of fidelity arises from the pack loyalty which binds the wild dog to the pack-leader or, respectively from the affection which the individual members of the pack feel for each other."*

CESAR MILLAN AND PACK LEADERSHIP

Pack leadership is the basis of Cesar Millan´s dog training methods. It is also the basis of training your puppy, together with canine conditioning and reward training. Don´t forget that the ultimate goal of all training is to teach your young dog how to live in your world and increase the likelihood that your life together will be long and happy for the both of you.

Dogs have been domesticated since prehistoric days. In fact, they were the first animals ever domesticated by humans. And precisely because of this long term of human companionship, your puppy needs you.

But why?

Primarily, because domesticated puppies depend on humans. As babies, they are not truly able to live by themselves in the wild. They are not adapted to living outside and foraging for food - especially not in a city or an urban environment.

Indeed, the dog you adopt today needs you and has many years to please you. And that desire to please his master is the reason that dogs are so easily trainable.

There's also another reason why your puppy needs you.

Dogs are pack animals, like horses and elephants. And as such they instinctively follow the leader of his pack. And in your puppy's case, as soon as he steps into your home, he joins your pack and therefore you become his natural pack leader.

As Konrad Lorenz stated:

> *"The relation of the dog to his master is similar to that of the wolf to the experienced pack-leader which conducts him across unknown territory."*

According to Cesar:

> *"Newborn puppies need to find a place*

or status within the pack. They don't get a name like we do because personality is something we create and only exists in our world. In the animal world there are two positions: the leader and the follower. Dogs are simple we make life complicated by misunderstanding what they need as a species. Dogs speak. Dogs communicate through constant energy. The pack leader always projects a calm, assertive energy."

NATURAL PACK LEADERSHIP

To fully understand the importance of becoming your puppy´s pack leader, you need to understand the basic teachings of dog psychology. The object of this science is the study of canines as pack animals and the role of pack leaders in dog society.

As Cesar claims:

"If you have a dog in your life, it is important to understand how to allow him to live in a balanced way and achieve a healthy state of mind. Dogs have found themselves in an odd predicament by living with humans. In the wild, dogs don't need humans to achieve balance. They have a

pack leader, work for food, and travel with the pack. But when we bring them into our world, we need to help them achieve balance by fulfilling their needs as nature intended them to be. How does this work? Through my fulfillment formula: exercise, then discipline, and finally, affection. As the human pack leader, you must set rules, boundaries, and limitations and always project a calm-assertive energy."

He defines dog psychology as the science of understanding dogs from a canine perspective rather than from a human perspective. According to him, *"the more you learn about dog psychology, the better you will be able to connect with your canine companion."*

Among other studies, dog psychology compares wild dogs in their natural habitats with domesticated dogs confined in human homes.

The following are its main findings:

PSYCHOLOGY OF DOGS IN THEIR PACKS:

*Most wolves and wild dogs live in natural groups or packs (although not all wolves live in groups and some do not live in groups all year round).

*The forming of a wolf pack appears to be a response to environmental pressures, with more grouping in times of duress, where it pays to cooperate for baby-sitting, hunting, scavenging, etc.

*Wolf packs and wild dog packs are led by dominant leaders followed by a group of submissive individuals.

*In the case of wolf packs and wild dog packs, the pack leaders are in control of the members of the pack and set their rules, being their dominance an intrinsic quality in them.

*Pack leaders don't project nervousness. They don't project panic. They don't project tension. Simply put, the pack leader is a calm, assertive presence that provides balance to the pack. They control everything and it´s not open to debate."

*Dogs think in terms of their natural instincts. They are built on instinct and that means they need to be fed, they need a place to sleep, and they need a strong pack that will help keep them safe and guide them.

*As adults, dogs look to their pack leader to create stability. They don't question the pack leader's position, and the pack leader doesn't look to the dogs to affirm his position. This is the natural balance of the pack.

*There can only be so many pack leaders, so most dogs are born submissive. This creates a balance in the pack that fosters healthy and happy dogs.

PSYCHOLOGY OF DOGS LIVING WITH HUMANS:

*When a dog comes to live with us, we become part of its pack and therefore must assume the role of pack leader or lose control.

*Unlike people who learn by listening, your puppy is much more attuned to nonverbal communication, from how you hold your body (especially in moments of tension or stress) to where you focus your eyes.

* When domestic dogs don´t find pack leaders at home, they constantly seek to increase their rank in the family and try to "dominate" us.

*Rehabilitating a dog is not about "fixing" it. It's about you, the owner, creating the intention for what you want, not what you're feeling. Dogs pick up on feelings of fear, doubt, or worry - and they will move to fill them by attempting to become dominant.

*Your puppy is a dog, bred to think like a dog and react naturally as an animal would. This means that rather than expecting your puppy to change for you, you need to change for your puppy.

*You are the source of your puppy's energy. You are the role model.

*Challenge the dog's mind -dogs want to know what to do with their lives. Let the dog work for your affection. Once in a calm-submissive state, your love will intensify those qualities in your puppy.

*Dogs need "on" and "off" time. Engage them fully in structured times together; then they can relax and avoid impatient or destructive behaviors.

*Don't expect more from your puppy(s) than your own children. Dogs need discipline, too. Give them rules, boundaries, and limitations as well as love.

*Giving your puppy love alone doesn't create balance in your puppy´s life. Be a pack leader.

*The more you learn about dog psychology, the better you will be able to connect with your canine companion!

BE THE PACK LEADER FROM DAY ONE

According to Cesar Millan, for your puppy to grow into a healthy, balanced dog, you must demonstrate leadership from day one:

"Puppies are naturally hard-wired to follow a pack leader. A

pack leader is, by definition, strong, stable and consistent; traits many new puppy owners forget around their dogs. I have had clients who are strong leaders in their jobs, but, when they come home, they turn to mush with their dogs. Then they come to me, puzzled as to why their dog won't behave."

He adds that that puppies can sense our confidence levels and will take control if they perceive us as weak. When dogs or puppies take control, bad behaviors, such as excessive barking, leash-pulling, or anxiety will develop. And this is why the most important thing you can do is to become your puppy's pack leader. This role doesn't begin when your dog is six months old or when he's bad. For your puppy to grow into a healthy, balanced dog, you must demonstrate leadership from day one.

IMPORTANT POINTS TO REMEMBER:

Here are some important points to remember in your role as pack leader:

When getting a new pet, make sure to set aside time every day to provide mental exercise by maintaining rules, boundaries and limitations.

When these needs are met, the affection you give to your dog will be channeled as a reward.

Create a schedule that includes a daily 45-minute power-walk in the morning. This is critical for your dog's health, both physical and mental.

Enlist your whole family in the process of bringing a new dog home. Discuss what their responsibilities will be before the puppy arrives.

Make sure you find a breed that fits your lifestyle. For example, more active breeds, like hunting and herding dogs, require more physical exercise to stay physically and mentally content.

Always walk out the door ahead of your dog when leaving the house. This will show your dog who is in the leadership role.

On walks, make sure that your dog is not in front of you, pulling you down the street. Instead, keep your dog to your side or behind you. This will also demonstrate to your dog that you are the alpha figure.

Give the puppy something to do before

you share food, water, toys or affection. This way the dog earns his treat. For example, have your puppy perform the Sit or Down command.

*Set aside a budget for unexpected circumstances, like medical bills and training classes. A healthy, well-trained dog makes a wonderful pet.

*A puppy will be set up to fail if his new family doesn't learn these lessons before he arrives. Remember, puppies don't crave a fancy treat or bed; they need you to become their stable pack leader to demonstrate love in a way they understand.

LESSON THREE

DOG CONDITIONING

ACCORDING TO THE AMERICAN POLICE-DOG TRAINER Deborah Palman, Master Trainer in Search and Rescue at International Police Work Dog Association and presently working for the Maine K-9 Services, the basic principles of training dogs are very simple:

> *"If you reward or positively reinforce*
> *the behaviors you want the dog to display,*
> *the frequency of these behaviors will*

increase. If you don't reinforce or discourage the behaviors you don't want, the frequency of these behaviors will decrease."

The practical application of these principles in training is what is known as "*dog conditioning*".

Truth is, when training you puppy, you will need to "condition" him to obey different commands. And by rewarding him you will effectively encourage the desired behaviors.

As Debora Palman states, the easiest dogs to train are those that value being rewarded. Those who don´t value the rewards a person can offer, become very difficult to train. Assuming that we are working with dogs that value food, toys, play, catching prey and social contact, training can progress by reinforcing behaviors that are desired.

BASIS OF DOG CONDITIONING

Dog conditioning was first studied by the Russian physician and researcher Ivan Pavlov, Novel prize winner in 1904. He was the first scientist to study the "learning process of dogs" and their "basic non-conscious instinctual type of learning". His "classic" conditioning experiment went as follows:

1: Pavlov took a dog and hooked him up to a mechanism that

measured the amount of saliva he produced.

2: Each time the dog was fed, Pavlov rang a bell just before he was given the food.

3: After several days doing this, the bell rang but the dog was not fed.

4: In spite of this, the dog salivated instinctively to the sound of the bell alone.

Pavlov concluded that through what he called the process of repeated "conditioning", the dog had effectively "learned" to salivate to the sound of the bell alone, just like our mouths water at the site, smell, or even memory of our favorite food.

A dog is said to be "conditioned" when he "learns" to "respond" automatically to some sort of "stimulus" with fear, joy, excitement, anticipation or with a "learned behavior", such as obeying a command or performing a dog trick.

Dog trainers around the world, including Cesar Millan, use commands and rewards for conditioning, acting like the bell and the food plate used in Pavlov's experiment and triggering predetermined responses in dogs practically at will.

OPERANT CONDITIONING

Considered the basis of animal training, the process known as "*operant conditioning*" was first outlined by the Pennsylvanian psychologist and behaviorist Burrhus F. Skinner, (1904–1990), who considered Ivan Pavlov´s classical conditioning too simplistic to explain complex behaviors.

Skinner based his new model on two basic modifiers of human and animal conduct.

*Reinforcers

*Punishments.

Although Skinner was openly against the use of harsh punishment, his model includes what he called "*positive*" and "*negative*" punishments. Presently most dog trainers are against the use of physical violence and never recommend it. Fortunately, this detestable practice has lost strength in recent decades, a gradual process that curiously began in the late 1800s, many years before Skinner and Pavlov, when the world's first dog-training books were published by the pioneers of *Positive Reward Training*, as the following lesson details.

POSITIVE AND NEGATIVE REINFORCERS

According to Skinner, there are two types of reinforcers: positive and negative, as explained below.

POSITIVE REINFORCERS: Positive reinforcers modify your dog's behavior by offering him a "*favorable reward or* *outcome*" each time he behaves properly. In order to be effective, however, the reward must be given immediately after the desired behavior. For example, by praising and rewarding your dog each time he obeys a new command, he will be more likely to repeat the same behavior in the near future. The most common rewards for dog are praise, food, petting and hugging, among others. Regarding the use of food when rewarding your dog, Skinner pointed out in "*The behavior of organisms*":

> "*A conditioned alimentary reflex is easily established in a hungry dog but slowly or not at all in one recently fed.*"

NEGATIVE REINFORCERS: Negative reinforcers does not involve punishment. They consist in the removal of an unfavorable or unpleasant outcome if your dog behaves properly. For example, a dog that obeys commands to avoid being punished. Sometimes, however, negative reinforcers backfire. Suppose your dog wants out, for example, and he starts barking loudly near the front door, like always. If you give in and open the door for him (like he wants), of course your dog will stop barking and leave! But by doing this, you will actually be reinforcing his loud barking and excited behavior each time he wants out!

In sum, when used properly, positive and negative reinforcers can both increase the likelihood that a specific behavior will later be repeated by your dog!

POSITIVE AND NEGATIVE PUNISHMENTS

Positive and negative punishments are used to make a dog less likely to repeat an unwanted behavior. They are just the opposite of positive and negative reinforcers, for they weaken or eliminate a specific behavior instead of strengthening it. Correction

POSITIVE PUNISHMENT: Though I don´t recommend the use of physical violence nor hurting animals in any possible way, it consists in giving your dog a disciplinary punishment, for example a spanking to weaken his undesired behavior. In certain cases you can use mild non-violent punishments to discipline your dog, as later described.

NEGATIVE PUNISHMENT: Negative punishment, on the other hand, consists in removing a favorable reward to weaken your dog's undesired behavior. For example, taking away your dog's favorite toy following an undesired behavior will surely help decrease that behavior.

"The kind of behavior that is correlated with specific eliciting stimuli may be called respondent behavior and a given correlation a respondent. The term is intended to carry the sense of a relation to a prior event. Such behavior as is not under this kind of control I shall call operant and any specific example an operant. The term refers to a posterior event..." **(B. F. Skinner)**

In short words, these are the basic principles of classical and operant conditioning:

Classical conditioning is the psychological process responsible of generating INVOLUNTARY responses in your dog.

For example, your dog sees you serving his dinner from across the room and starts salivating as soon as he sees you with his food, even before taking a step closer.

Operant conditioning is the psychological process responsible of generating VOLUNTARY responses in your dog.

For example, you train your dog to do a double summersault and each time he succeeds you give him a treat and pat his head.

CONDITIONING EXAMPLE: THE "COME" COMMAND

The first and most basic training command you need to teach your puppy is the "Come" command. If you can, teach him this command today.

This command can be used for various reasons.

For example, if you take your dog for a walk and you let him off the leash, then you will be able to call him back. Teaching him this command only requires basic conditioning techniques, including rewards and repetition.

A well trained dog that comes when called can safely be taken out to play in the local park, at the beach, on the hiking trail, or anywhere else the owner and dog may wish to go. Coming when called is a vital skill that every dog must learn, both for its own safety and that of those around it.

On the other hand, a disobedient dog that refuses to come when called could easily be hit by a car, get into a fight with another dog, or suffer a variety of other bad experiences.

To condition your puppy to obey the "Come" command take the following steps:

*Get a toy in one hand and a treat in the other.

*Simply walk by your puppy or walk away from him.

*Then hold out the toy and excitingly say the command "Come!"

*When your puppy comes to you, praise him and give a doggie treat. Do this each time he succeeds!

*Do this several times a day and always use the same command for come and reward him properly.

*In two or three days your puppy will have learned to obey your command.

Remember: This is a great way to teach him, but don´t forget to have lots of long breaks so he doesn't get bored and stop enjoying it… and don't forget giving him treats!

When teaching the dog to come on command, it is vital that the dog be consistently rewarded every single time he does as the owner wants. A reward can be a doggie treat, but it can also be as simple as a pat on the head, a "good boy", or a scratch behind the ears.

Of course, treat based rewards are appreciated as well, and many dogs are highly food motivated and respond quickly to this type of training. The key is to be consistent.

Many dog owners fail to recognize the importance of having a dog that comes when called until there is a problem, such as the collar or leash breaking, or the dog tearing free to chase a person or another animal.

These situations can be dangerous for the dog, the owner and other members of the community. In areas where there is a lot of vehicular traffic, the situation could even prove fatal to the puppy.

LESSON FOUR

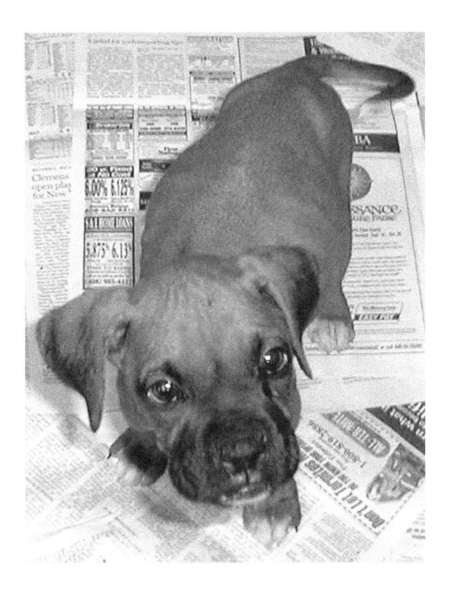

PREPARING FOR HOUSE TRAINING

NOW THAT YOU KNOW THE BASICS of pack leadership and dog conditioning, you are ready to begin your puppy's house

31

training, undoubtedly the first and most important part of training any dog to be a valued part of the family.

This lesson will tell you all you need to do before you get your puppy, as you prepare for his arrival. And this means from buying the specific supplies he will be needing, to setting up his training and potty areas.

As with many other aspects of dog training, the best way to house train a puppy is to use the dog's own nature to your benefit.

The great thing about dogs, and the thing that can make house training much easier, is that they are instinctively very clean animals.

A puppy will instinctively move away from its bed to urinate and go potty. This is because dogs prefer not to soil the areas where they sleep and eat.

"When puppies are first born," Cesar explains, *"they eat and they relieve themselves inside the den, but the mother always cleans them. There is never a scent of urine or feces where the puppies eat, sleep, and live. When they get old enough, they learn to use outside areas as they imitate their mother. In this way, all dogs become conditioned never to eliminate in their dens."*

Dogs are also very good at developing habits regarding where they like to urinate and defecate. For example, dogs that are used to eliminating on concrete or gravel will prefer to eliminate there rather than on grass or dirt. It is possible to use these natural canine habits when house training your dog!

One thing I recommend doing as soon as you get your puppy is getting him and ID plaque for his collar and implanting him a microchip, which is a safe and permanent way of identifying your dog. The procedure is quite simple: A very small electronic chip is implanted through a needle under the skin in the back of your dog's neck/shoulders. And if by any chance your dog is ever lost or injured, then a vet or council pound will be able to scan the dog and contact you.

SETTING UP THE TRAINING AREA

The first ste p in house training your puppy is to set up your training area.

A small, confined space such as a bathroom, or part of a kitchen or garage, works best as a training area. Make sure to puppy proof the area (puppy proofing a room is very similar to baby proofing a room, since puppies chew on everything)

It is important for the owner to spend as much time in the training area with his or her dog as possible. It is also important for the owner to play with the dog in the training area, and to let the dog eat and sleep in that area.

Don't forget that moving into a new house can be a traumatic experience for your puppy. So make the training area nice and appealing to the dog.

The dog should be provided with a special bed or towel in the training area where he can lie down and sleep, preferably within a large box, crate or kennel.

For top training, get a crate or kennel.

It should be large enough for your dog to sit up, stand, and turn around. Too large of a crate is not going to make your dog feel secure and too small will be uncomfortable.

When you are not actively engaged in playing with or walking your puppy should be confined to the training area or in his crate. This includes overnight and while you are not home.

Since your puppy will likely get larger you may have to invest in successively larger kennels. Maintain them well and you should be able to sell them online or at a yard sale. Your local dog shelter would probably love a donation of an old kennel if you are so inclined.

After the dog has gotten used to sleeping in the bed, you can move it around the house, relocating it from room to room.

In any case, remember not to confine your puppy to the training area exclusively. You will also need to take him outside. Doing outdoor activities together is one of the wonderful things about having a puppy. Not only will this help him feel good, but it will also strengthen his bond with you. Certain sports, however, should only be practiced by dogs once they have finished growing. Dog training clubs are an excellent way to teach him a few simple exercises that will be useful when playing these sports in the future.

Young puppies generally get all the exercise they need by racing around the garden and playing, but once your puppy is fully vaccinated you can take him for short walks away from home. This will help to familiarise him with different environments.

Puppies develop both mentally and physically at an astounding rate. The age at which 'real' exercise should begin varies from breed to breed, as does the amount. Your vet will be able to advise you.

In any case, playing with your puppy is vital in his socialization and upbringing. Dogs can learn through play, helping them to refine their socially interactive behavior with their owners. Make exercise fun by taking along a ball or a Frisbee, so that you can play games. Avoid small balls which he could swallow, or sticks which could lodge in his throat and injure him.

GETTING SUPPLIES FOR YOUR PUPPY

When you prepare the training area, you will also need to

purchase the different products and supplies your puppy will need in his new home.

For training purposes, perhaps the most important is a sufficient supply of doggie treats, for you will need it for housebreaking and other basic behavioral training.

Avoid giving your puppy with rawhide strips, for they can be very toxic for young puppies and thus shouldn´t be given until they are adults.

Apart from biscuits and homemade treats, there are all sorts of different kinds available.Make sure to get ones that your little puppy can handle chewing up. You might even cut up the treats into small, bite sized pieces.

There are also treat bags that you can purchase that will clip to your belt or pocket, but a sandwich bag that is sealed works just as well. You probably do not want to just keep them in your pocket because the dog will smell them and will not leave you alone.

So get a large supply and a wide variety of treats!

What else should you get for your puppy?

According to the San Francisco dog trainer Patricia Halloran, apart from doggie treats, the following are some of the basic objects you'll need to get before your young pet arrives:

*Water bowl

*Food dish

*Start or puppy dog food (no by-products, fillers or meal).

*Leash/harness or collar (a collar is all right, but a harness can be easier on the dog's neck and back)

*Chewable toys (balls and hard chew, squeaky, stuffed toys. It is very important to have toys available to chew for your puppy will be teething for several months. Also get a Frisbee. Never punish the dog for chewing on you or on a wrong object. Instead, immediately replace the object with a chewable toy and give him lots of praise)

*Teething ring (To help with teething discomfort/pain, get a baby's teething ring and follow instructions. Basically fill with water and put in freezer. This will soothe your dog's little mouth.

*Crate (See the lesson on crate training

for details. Never use the crate to punish your dog. You want him to view his crate as a safe place, cozy and secure. You can also line it with fleecy crate pads so it's very cozy and soft to lie on).

*Bed/Blanket (Your dog deserves his own little bed and blanket for comfort and warmth. You can also use a soft towel for him to sleep)

*Soft brush (kitty brushes are good at first)

*Soft small slicker brush

*Comb (never pull roughly through hair, gently hold ear leather and comb slowly; you don't want to frighten your dog by pulling out knots. If some hair is too knotted up, use scissors and carefully cut off the knot -much better than pulling).

*Doggie tooth paste (you can use CET and put it on your index finger and gently rub it over your puppy's teeth, getting to the back. It tastes good to them and can save tooth problems worry and expense.

Other grooming items you should consider getting include:

*Blow dryer

*Conditioning spray

*Cotton balls

*Ear cleaning solution

*Nail clippers

*Scissors

*Shampoo and conditioner

*Styptic powder

*Towels

Remember to get these products before your puppy comes home and to set them up in advance!

SETTING UP THE POTTY AREA

Another important stage of house training is to set up the potty or toilet area for the dog. Initially, if your puppy is too young to go outside every time he needs to go, it is best to set a provisional potty area in your puppy's training area.

At first, the puppy may eliminate in the training area, but once the dog has recognized it as his or her own space, he or she will be reluctant to soil it. He will then need to learn to go outside.

You can also teach your puppy to go outside directly, especially if you live in a house and not an apartment and have a private yard he can go to.

In any case, it is important for your puppy to have access to this place every time he needs to evacuate. It is also important for you, as his master and pack-leader to accompany your puppy each time he goes, at least during the first few days and he gets into the habit of going where you want him to go. This will ensure that the dog uses only the established area.

In the next lesson we will see how you can easily train your puppy to go potty where you want him to. This is a very important part of your training, because at first he will not know the difference between the potty area and the rest of your house.

LESSON FIVE

POTTY TRAINING

EASILY THE MOST IMPORTANT and first thing you will do is potty training.

Your puppy knows no difference between the inside of your house and the backyard. As far as they are concerned there are very few places that are not acceptable place to pee or poop.

It should be relatively easy for you to train your dog to do potty where he should if you are willing to follow the basic steps given in this book. And as you begin this process you may have to cut those close and cuddly ties you have already established with your puppy.

To housebreak a puppy you will need to keep him confined to a small area, in your home. While this may seem like punishment remember that dogs were once den dwelling animals.

They like their crate or doghouse, since it makes them feel secure.

For top training, get a crate or kennel for your puppy. It should be large enough for your dog to sit up, stand, and turn around. Too large of a crate is not going to make your dog feel secure and too small will be uncomfortable.

Since your dog will likely get larger you may have to invest in successively larger kennels. Maintain them well and you should be able to sell them online or at a yard sale. Your local dog shelter would probably love a donation of an old kennel if you are so inclined.

When you are not actively engaged in playing with or walking your puppy he should be in a crate. This includes overnight and while you are not home.

The puppy should not expect, nor should he be given free run of your home. This will give him an early sense of dominance and make it harder to train him. In addition, most dogs will not eliminate in their kennels, so you reduce the risk of an in home accident.

Some people, especially apartment dwellers with small dogs, use pee pee pads. It seems a little gross, but can be a necessity if you live in an apartment where going downstairs constantly can be a hassle.

There are some good grass beds available that are an alternative to pee pee pads. They are much more appealing to look at or smell.

This is also a good choice if your puppy will use your balcony to relieve himself. Neither of these are good options if your puppy will eventually be a medium to large sized dog.

Big dogs equal big puddles and big poops, the pads and grass beds are not large enough to handle it.

GETTING YOUR PUPPY TO GO POTTY

A set feeding schedule makes the house training process a lot easier for both the owner and the dog. Feeding the dog on a regular basis will also create a regular schedule for the dog's toilet habits.

It is also important to always feed and give water to your puppy at the same time. Some people choose to feed dogs twice a day, others only once. Your puppy will let you know which it prefers.

Like Cesar explains, *"another built-in plus when it comes to housebreaking is our puppy's digestive tract, which is extremely quick and efficient: Five to 30 minutes after the puppy eats, she'll want to defecate."*

Each time you feed him, your puppye should be given a set amount of time, maybe fifteen to twenty minutes to eat and then the food should be taken away. And then you should immediately take him to go potty.

Once you know when your dog is likely to need to defecate, it will be simple to guide the dog to the established area. With a consistent eating schedule, and your attention to the clock, this won´t be hard to do.

If your puppy is only a few days or weeks old, take him to the potty area every 45 minutes to an hour. And when you are not at home or cannot supervise the puppy, you must be sure the puppy cannot make a mistake. This means confining the puppy to his crate or the training area.

Fact is, puppies need to go potty quite often. Very young puppies need to almost every hour!

The rule of thumb is that a puppy can hold it for one hour for every month of age plus one hour. For example, if your dog is two months old he should be able to hold it for three hours. However, this does not mean you should wait three hours before taking him out!

Based on this formula, you need to determine how often your puppy needs to go potty. Depending on his s age, try to come up with a schedule.

For example: If your puppy is two months old, he will need to go potty every two and a half to three hours.

Taking this into account, before beginning your pupy´s training you must first determine the exact time he last went potty and calculate the approximate time when he will need to go again.

Let´s say your untrained puppy just went potty on the living room rug or kitchen floor. Then approximately two hours from now, you should lock yourself with him in the training area and wait till he feels the urge to go.

If he positions himself to go potty and is not in the potty area, interrupt him by holding him up in your arms and distracting him. Then immediately take him to the potty area and keep him there by blocking his moves or grabbing him and placing him back.

Sooner or later he will feel the urge again and take position.

That´s when you need to use a command or cue phrase of your choice, like "Go Potty" or "Potty". By repeating this command each time he goes potty, it will get engrained in your puppy´s mind and he will react to it in a conditioned way throughout his life.

Make sure the command word is brief and that everyone in the household who will take the dog out uses the same cue phrase.

Repeat the command while the puppy goes potty, until he is completely finished.

Once he is done it is very important to condition your puppy by praising him, giving him affection and rewarding him with a doggie treat.

If he does not go potty within five minutes put him in his kennel. Wait fifteen to twenty minutes and try it again.

At first, you will need to repeat this process every few hours, for several days, until your puppy learns the lesson,

Each time your puppy has a successful potty venture praise him, reward him with a doggie treat and allow him to have some supervised play time.

This is vital to condition your puppy by repetition and make him obey his master´s command.

As Cesar claims, "*done correctly, housebreaking should not be a turbulent production but just a matter of putting a little extra work into getting your puppy on a schedule during the first weeks after he arrives at your home.*"

ADVANCED POTTY TRAINING

Once the dog is consistently eliminating in the toilet area and not soiling the training area, it is time to extend that training area to the rest of the home and outside, which will be his regular potty area in the future.

However, this process should be done slowly.

In the case of extending the training area to the rest of the home, be sure to start out with one room and slowly expand to the rest of the house.

The area should only be extended once you are sure of the dog's ability to control its bladder and bowels.

When you first expand the training area to a single room, let the dog eat, play and sleep in that room, but only when supervised.

When it is not possible to supervise the dog, place it back in the original training area. Then, after the dog has accepted the room as an extension of the original training area, the area can be extended.

If this process is too lengthy for your needs, it can be speeded up, but it is important to proceed cautiously.

In fact, it is much easier to take your time up front than to retrain a problem later!

If you choose to take him outside, always take him to the same place. In any case, to speed up the process, make sure to praise and reward the dog with a treat each and every time he uses the established toilet area.

To train your dog to go potty outside, Cesar recommends the following:

*First thing every morning, bring your puppy outside to the same general area.

*It is important to remain consistent throughout the process so your puppy can learn the habit.

*Once your puppy has successfully gone outside, it is important to reward the good behavior. It doesn't have to be a big, loud celebration, but a simple quiet approval or a treat can get the message across of a job well done.

*Never punish your puppy for an accident or do anything to create a negative association with her bodily functions. Stay calm and assertive and quietly remove the puppy to the place where you want him to go.

What happens if you do not succeed?

Above all, if your puppy does not learn to go potty where you want him to, do not despair.

Some dogs take longer than others. With few exceptions, if you follow the instructions contained in this book, you should have your puppy trained within a few more days.

You could also adjust your schedule so that it better suits his needs.

Also, never demean or punish your puppy for his "accidents". They are just that, accidents. He is not purposely disobeying you.

Avoid the cruel and old fashioned technique of rubbing your puppy´s nose in the mess they have made. This will only teach him to fear and mistrust you. Punishment of any form will not help with your relationship with your new young pet.

All your puppy wants is your love and approval, the more of that you are able to give to him the more he will behave in a positive manner.

Even the best trained dogs have accidents while they are young, so be patient. And don´t punish your dog for his mistakes. Punishment will only confuse the puppy and slow down the house training process.

In the meantime, my advice is to keep a good supply of floor and carpet cleaner on hand to deal with any messes the puppy might make in those first few years.

LESSON SIX

DO'S AND DON'TS OF HOUSE TRAINING

HOUSE TRAINING A PUPPY is very important for the well-being of both the puppy and the owner.

The number one reason that dogs are surrender to animal shelters is problems with inappropriate elimination, so it is easy to see why proper house training is such an important consideration.

It is important to establish proper potty habits when the puppy is young, since these habits can last a lifetime, and be very hard to break once they are established.

It is also very important for the owner to house break the puppy properly. In most cases, true house training cannot begin until the puppy is six months old.

Puppies younger than this generally lack the bowel and bladder control that is needed for true house training.

Puppies younger than six months should be confined to a small, puppy proofed room when the owner cannot supervise them. The entire floor of the room should be covered with newspapers or similar absorbent materials, and the paper changed every time it is soiled.

As the puppy gets older, the amount of paper used can be reduced as the puppy begins to establish a preferred toilet area.

It is this preferred toilet area that will form the basis of later house training.

THE DO'S OF HOUSE TRAINING YOUR PUPPY:

*Always provide the puppy with constant, unrestricted access to the established toilet area.

*Always provide a toilet area that does not resemble anything in your home. Training the puppy to eliminate on concrete, blacktop, grass or dirt is a good idea. The puppy should never be encouraged to eliminate on anything that resembles the hardwood flooring, tile or carpet he may encounter in a home.

*Praise and reward your puppy every time he eliminates in the established toilet area. The puppy must learn to associate pottying in the established areas with good things, like treats, toys and praise from his owner.

*Always keep a set schedule when feeding your puppy, and provide constant access to fresh, clean drinking water. A consistent feeding schedule equals a consistent toilet schedule.

*Using a crate can be a big help in helping a puppy develop self-control. The concept behind crate training is that the puppy will not want to potty in his bed area.

*And finally, it is important to be patient when house training a puppy. House training can take as long as several months, but it is much easier to house train right the first time than to retrain a problem dog.

THE DON'TS OF HOUSE TRAINING YOUR PUPPY:

*Never reprimand or punish the puppy for mistakes. Punishing the puppy will only cause fear and confusion.

*Do not leave food out for the puppy all night long. Keep to a set feeding schedule in order to make the dog's toilet schedule as consistent as possible.

*Do not give the puppy the run of the house until he has been thoroughly house trained.

LESSON SEVEN

HOUSE TRAINING ISSUES

THE BEST HOUSE TRAINING uses the dogs own instincts to avoid soiling its bed to train the dog where and where not to eliminate.

That is the basis behind crate training, in which the dog is confined to its crate in the absence of the owner, and den training, in which the dog is confined to a small area of the home. In essence, the crate, or the room, becomes the dog's den.

Dogs are naturally very clean animals, and they try their best to avoid using their dens as toilets.

This type of training usually works very well, both for puppies and for older dogs. Problems with this type of toilet training are usually the result of not understanding the signals the dog is sending, not being consistent with feeding times, or trying to rush the process.

While the house training process can be sped up somewhat by consistently praising the dog and rewarding it for toileting in the proper place, some dogs cannot be rushed through this important process. It is always best to house train the dog properly the first time than to go back and retrain a problem dog.

If the dog continues to soil the den area after house training, the most likely reason is that the owner has left the dog in the den for too long. Another reason may be that the den area is too large. In this case, the best strategy is to make the den area smaller or to take the dog to the toilet area more frequently.

If the dog soils the bed that has been provided in the den area, it is most likely because the owner has left the dog there for too long, and the dog had an understandable accident. Or it could be that the dog has not yet adopted this area as the bed. In addition, urinary tract infections and other medical conditions can also cause dogs to soil their beds. It is important to have the dog thoroughly checked out by a veterinarian to rule out any medical problems.

One other reason for house training accidents that many people overlook is boredom. Dogs who are bored often drink large amounts of water and therefore must urinate more frequently than you might think. If you notice your dog consuming large amounts of water, be sure to take the dog to the established toilet area more often, and provide the dog with toys and other distractions to eliminate boredom.

Boredom is the root cause of many dog behavior problems, not only house training issues. Chewing and other destructive behaviors are also often caused by boredom and separation anxiety.

Other problems with house training can occur when the dog's den is not properly introduced. In some cases dogs can react to the den as if it is a prison or a punishment.

Those dogs may exhibit signs of anxiety, such as whining, chewing and excessive barking. It is important for the dog to feel secure in its den, and to think of it as a home and not a cage.

The best way to house train a puppy or dog, or to re-house train a problem dog, is to make you aware of the dog's habits and needs. Creating a healthy, safe sleeping and play area for your dog, as well as a well-defined toilet area, is important for any house training program.

House training is not always an easy process, but it is certainly an important one. The number one reason that dogs are surrendered to animal shelters is problems with inappropriate elimination, so a well-structured house training program can literally be a lifesaver for your dog.

MORE ON HOUSE TRAINING

House training is not always the easiest thing to do, and some dogs tend to be much easier to house train than others. It is important, however to be patient, consistent and loving as you train your dog.

A rushed, frightened or intimidated dog will not be able to learn the important lessons of house training. Once you have gained your puppy's love and respect, however, you will find that house training your puppy is easier than you ever expected.

House training is one of those issues that every dog owner must grapple with. In most cases house training is the first major milestone in the relationship between owner and dog, and it can sometimes be difficult and confusing for owner and dog alike.

The best house training procedures are those that use the dog's own instincts to the owner's advantage. These strategies take into account the dog's reluctance to soil the spots where he eats and sleeps. This is the concept behind den training and crate training. Dogs are very clean animals, and in nature they always avoid using their dens as potty areas.

These kinds of natural training methods generally work very

well, for both puppies and older dogs. Naturally, older, larger dogs will need a larger area for their den, and crate training is generally best used for puppies and small dogs.

When house training a puppy, however, it is important to pay close attention to the signals he sending. It is also important to be consistent when it comes to feeding times, and to provide the dog with ready access to the toilet area you establish on a regular basis.

It is important as well to never try to rush the process of house training. While some dogs are naturally easier to train, most puppies and adult dogs will experience at least one or two slip ups during the house training process.

When these accidents occur, it is important to not get mad and punish the dog. Accidents during house training usually mean that the owner is trying to move too fast, or that the dog has been left alone for too long. In this case, it is best to just take a step back and start the process again.

It is also important for the owner to reward the dog enthusiastically when it does its business in the appointed area. The dog should learn to associate doing its business in its potty area with good things like treats, rewards and praise.

During the house training process, the den area starts out very small, often as small as half of a small room in the beginning. As the dog learns to control his bladder and bowels better, and the owner learns to anticipate the dog's toilet needs, the den area can be slowly expanded.

It is important not to make the den area too large too soon.

The den area must be expanded slowly in order for the house training process to move along smoothly.

It is important for the dog to be properly introduced to its den.

Many dogs, particularly those who have never been confined before, such as those who have spent their lives as outdoor dogs, may react to the den area as if it is a prison, and constantly whine, cry and try to escape the den. It is important that the dog learn to accept its den as a home and not a cage.

One problem many dog owners overlook when house training a dog is that of boredom. Boredom is actually the root cause of many behavior problems in dogs, including chewing and other destructive behaviors. Boredom can also be the root cause of problems with house training.

Dogs that are bored often consume large amounts of water during the day, and this excess water consumption can lead to the need to urinate often, even in its den area. Since soiling the den area goes against the dog's nature, he can quickly become confused and frightened, thereby setting the house training program back even further.

To prevent the dog from becoming bored when you are away from home, be sure to provide him with lots of different kinds of toys, as well as a safe and secure place to sleep. In addition, a vigorous period of play time can help the dog sleep while you are away. In addition, playing with the dog in its den area will help him bond with this area and recognize it as a safe, secure home.

LESSON EIGHT

BASIC TRAINING COMMANDS

NOW THAT YOU HAVE LEARNED the basics of dog training, you should take your time to teach your puppy a few basic commands. This will certainly make his life easier, as well as yours.

A well-trained dog makes for a happy home. Your dog does not have to do a bunch or tricks nor does he have to be perfect. You are probably not training a show dog or a guide dog so you do not have to stress out about making him behave perfectly.

Try to focus your energy on key behavior like housebreaking, responding to commands, and waling on a leash. As you get to know your puppy better you will find out what he is good at and can expand on those good behaviors and learn to manage the unwanted behavior.

People often ask Cesar at what age they should start puppy training. The answer is immediately!

According to the celebrated dog breeder Carmen Battaglia, "all dogs can benefit from obedience training as early as seven weeks and also when the puppy enters its new home."

Most puppy training can be done on your own, right in your own home. There are dog training classes that you can take to help you get started. These can be good, but are only the beginning of the training process.

Your new dog will need to continued attention and behavior in order for him to be the best dog that he can be.

USING BASIC COMMANDS

The first thing you need to do is teach your puppy his name. Obedience training begins with 'attention' or 'your name means look at me'. Start by simply saying your puppy's name whenever he looks at you. In this way you are labelling the behaviour of looking at you with your puppy's name.

The next step is to call your puppy's name and see if he turns to look at you – if he does immediately reward with praise, a treat or a game.

If he doesn't, use a prompt first such as clapping hands or making a funny noise, when your puppy does look immediately say his name and reward.

By using a prompt to get your puppy's attention instead of repeating his name over and over again, you avoid accidentally training your puppy to ignore his name. Always follow a response to his name with a positive reward.

Once your dog learns his name, you can start teaching him his first vocal commands.

Try to always use one-word commands and always pronounce the voice signal with the same tone and inflection after gaining your puppy's attention by saying his name.

For example: "Snoopy, come!" or "Fido, sit!"

Start out your puppy´s basic training by teaching him only one command at a time. Do not overload your puppy!

Begin by teaching your puppy a first command. Then work on it for a few days using little 5 minute sessions. Remember that puppies have a very short attention span that may vary from two to five minutes, depending on the breed.

Once he learns the first command, you can teach your puppy another one. And after he learns the second, you will be able to practice both two and so forth.

Don't get carried away with the number of vocal commands you create. Take it slow.

Remember: One syllable words work best. Pups and dogs respond easily to one syllable words. Remember they do not understand the meaning of words or sentences. However they do recognize sounds and associate them with specific behaviors.

Dogs can learn a lot if the commands are simple and consistent. Remember this rule. "Learning is not portable". If a command is learned in the house, take the pup outside, to the park and shopping center and repeat the same command. It will not be long before the pup/dog learns what the command means regardless of the location.

You can also teach your puppy to obey different hand signals.

In this case, just like Pavlov´s bell, your puppy can trigger a desired response by showing him a specific position of your hand.

Among the most common hand signals is the following:

Place your flat hand in front of your puppy´s head while saying "Sit", before pulling it up into a loose fist. Another common practice is placing your left hand above your puppy's head, palm toward the floor, and then lowering your hand towards the floor while saying "down".

In any case, using a specific hand motion can be an effective way of training a dog to respond to different stimuli.

When training your puppy, start out by using voice and hand signal commands and eventually you can wean your puppy off the vocal command so that he responds to the hand signal alone. This is most useful for giving long-distance orders

It is also recommended to give hand signals in front of and above the dog's head as that is their best field of vision.

In some ways training a puppy is easier because he is essentially a "blank slate", untroubled by past training techniques and other issues. But did you know that in some aspects the puppy can be more difficult to train than an older dog? For example, one challenge to training a new puppy is that puppies are more easily distractible than adolescent and adult dogs.

Everything is new to a puppy, and every new experience provides a new chance for distraction. For this reason, it is best to keep training sessions short when working with a puppy, and to end each training sessions on a positive note.

BENEFITS OF TRAINING YOUR PUPPY

There are many reasons for pet owners to want a calm, obedient and faithful puppy. For one thing, obedient and trained puppies are happier dogs, less likely to get into tussles with people or with other dogs.

Another reason is that many human communities require that the dogs living in their neighborhoods be well trained.

This is especially true for many breeds thought to have aggression and behavior problems, such as Rottweilers or Pit Bulls, like my own dog Brutus.

Of course, basic training will also make your dog a much better companion -especially in households where there are young children.

Many studies have also shown that proper dog training makes a big impact when it comes to cutting down behavior problems.

When considering training your own dog, or having someone else help you train it, there are certain basic commands that must be mastered in order for a dog to be considered truly trained.

The basic obedience commands that every dog must know are:

*Come

*Sit

*Stay

*Heel

*No

*Down

*Off

*Stop

*Stop & Sit

These commands form the basis of basic obedience training, and it is vital that you and your dog master these commands.

I already explained how to teach your puppy the "Come" command. In the following pages I will teach you the rest of the basic commands you should teach him to assure him a harmonic and happy life.

LESSON NINE

THE SIT COMMAND

THE SIT COMMAND is a vital link in the chain of dog training.

Teaching a puppy to sit on command, using voice commands alone, will form the groundwork of much future training, so it is important for the dog to master this vital skill.

Getting your puppy to sit is a bit harder than getting him to come. But not that much. Again, it only requires basic dog conditioning and repetition.

Once you have mastered the "Come" command, follow these steps to teach your puppy to sit:

*Call your puppy to you using the come command.

*Place your hand on the end of his back (lower back) and say the command "SIT".

*Gently push down on his backside until he sits.

*Give him a doggie treat and a lot of praise.

If you want him to sit longer just delay giving him the treat and the praise, get him to sit but take your time bending down to him and feeding him his titbit.

LESSON TEN

THE STAY COMMAND

THE STAY COMMAND, just like the sit command, is a vital building block to other, more advanced training.

For instance, the stay command is vital to teaching the dog to come when called, which is in turn vital to off leash work.

The stay command can be made into an extension of the sit command. Have your dog sit, and while he is sitting, slowly back away. If the puppy begins to follow you, as he probably will it first, come back to the dog and ask him to sit again.

Repeat the process until you can reach the end of the leash

73

without your dog getting up from a sitting position.

After the puppyis reliably staying where you indicate, you can try dropping the leash and backing further away. It will probably take the dog some time to reliably stay where he is put without becoming distracted.

LESSON ELEVEN

THE HEEL COMMAND

ONE OF THE MOST BASIC commands of all is the "Heel" command.

Teaching a dog to heel is one of the first steps in teaching the dog to walk properly on the leash. The proper place for the puppy to walk is at your side, neither lagging behind nor straining to get ahead.

If your dog begins to forge ahead on the lead, gently tug on the leash. This will cause the training collar to tighten and give the dog a gentle reminder to fall back into line.

If the dog begins to lag behind, gently urge him forward. A lure or toy is a good tool for the puppythat constantly lags behind.

Once the dog is consistently walking at your side, try to change your pace and encouraging the dog to match his pace with yours.

It should always be the dog who adjusts his pace to you; you should never adjust your pace to meet the needs of the dog.

LESSON TWELVE

THE NO COMMAND

THE WORD "NO" is an important one for your dog to learn, and one you may be using a lot as training begins.

It is important that the puppylearn to respond to a sharp "No" promptly and obediently.

To train your puppy to obey this command, you can use the different "no-mark" techniques recommended by Cesar, including the "tsch" sound, hand poking, and body blocking, among others.

LESSON THIRTEEN

THE OFF COMAND

THE OFF COMMAND is just as vital to as the other commands, and it forms the basis for later training, especially when training the puppy, not to chase people, cars, bikes, cats, etc.

For instance, when training a dog to remain still when a bicycle goes by, the owner would stand with the dog calmly on the leash.

If the puppybegins to strain against the leash, the owner sharply issues an "Off" command accompanied by a tug of the leash.

Eventually the dog will learn to respond to the voice command alone.

LESSON FOURTEEN

THE STOP COMMAND

LEARNING THE "STOP" command is quite simple:

*As you walk alongside your dog, stop abruptly and say the command "Stop".

*If your dog does not stop when you do, give a sharp tug on the leash to remind the dog and repeat the command "No". Many dogs will instinctively stop when you do, while others need to be reminded through the use of the leash and the training collar. Repeat this procedure over and over until your puppy understands what is expected of him.

*After learning the "Stop" command, you can combine it with the "Sit" command as follows:

*Once your puppy has stopped by your side, you can urge him to sit by pushing gently on his hindquarters. It is important not to use too much pressure, or to push him down abruptly. Doing so could f-righten, or even injure the dog. Rather, apply a steady downward pressure. Most dogs will recognize this as a sit command. It is important to say the word sit as you do this.

*Repeat this procedure a few times by walking, stopping and sitting your dog.

*After a few repetitions, the dog will probably begin to sit down on his own every time he stops

*It is important to say the command words "Stop" and "Sit" each time, so that the dog will eventually learn to respond to voice commands alone.

LESSON FIFTEEN

LEASH/COLLAR PUPPY TRAINING

AS CESAR HAS REPEATED in many of his television episodes, a well trained dog is one who will walk at his owner's side on a loose lead, neither dropping behind nor charging ahead.

He also claims that both leash/collar training and reward training have been around for a very long time, and they have proven their effectiveness over time. They are the best ways to accomplish basic dog conditioning, particularly in situations where the puppy must have a high level of reliability.

For instance, dogs that have an important job to do, such as rescue dogs, police dogs and guard dogs, generally benefit highly from leash and collar training.

In leash and collar training, varying degrees of force can be used, ranging from slight prompts with the lead to very harsh corrections.

The amount of correction used should be appropriate to the situation, since using too much correction, or too little, will be ineffective.

Always keep in mind that the leash and the training collar are the most basic pieces of equipment used in training a puppy as well as an adult dog. Using them properly is vital to successful dog training!

The training collar is designed to apply a specific amount of pressure each time the leash is tightened.

The amount of pressure put on the leash controls the amount of pressure placed on the training collar, and the pressure can be adjusted according to how the dog responds.

How each puppy responds to training with the leash and training collar is quite variable. Some barely react the first time they encounter a collar and leash, while others fight this strange contraption with all their might.

It is important to recognize how your own dog reacts, and to adapt your training program as needed.

In a collar and leash based dog training program, first the dog is taught a particular behavior, generally with the leash. After he has demonstrated that it understands the command, the leash is then used to correct the dog if it disobeys, or when it makes a mistake.

The leash is the main form of controlling and communicating with the dog in leash and collar training.

When using leash and collar training, the puppy must be trained to trust the handler and accept his or her directions without question.

In order for the puppy to be fully trained, the handler must demonstrate the ability to place the dog into a posture or position he or she does not want to take.

This does not mean using force, but it does generally require some level of physical manipulation. This manipulation is most easily and safely done using the main tool of leash and collar training – the leash.

It is important for every dog trainer to understand that the leash is simply a tool. While the leash is an important tool in this form of training, it is important for the dog trainer to be able to eventually achieve the same results using whatever tools are at hand.

Even when the only tools at hand are the owner's body and skill, the dog should be willing to obey.

Creating a leader/follower relationship between handler and dog is still very important, and it is important to use the leash as a tool and not a crutch. A properly trained puppy should be willing to obey whether the leash is present or not.

THE RIGHT COLLAR AND LEASH

The first part of training with collar and leash, of course, is to purchase a quality, well-made training collar that will fit your puppy properly.

There are many types of training collars and leashes on the market. The most important thing is to choose one that is sturdy and well made. The last thing you want to do is chase your dog down after he has broken his collar.

It is important that the collar be neither too light nor too heavy, neither too thin nor too thick.

A collar that is too light for the puppy can be easily broken, while a collar that is too heavy may be uncomfortable for him to wear. It is also important that the width of the color be appropriate for the size of the dog.

Determining the proper length of the collar is relatively easy. Simply wrap a tape measure or a string lightly around the puppy neck to get an accurate measurement. It is important that the tape measure not be tight, just slightly snug.

Most collars are sized in two inch increments, so you may have to round up to get a properly sized collar. For instance, if the dog has a 13" neck, you would buy a 14" collar, and so on.

It is important that the chain that attaches to the collar be placed at the top of the dog's neck. That is where the training collar is designed to apply the best pressure.

The ability to apply varying degrees of pressure, and to relieve that pressure instantly, is what makes a training collar such an effective tool.

After you have purchased the perfect collar, the next step is to put it on the dog and allow him to wear it around the house. Do not be dismayed if the dog whines, paws at the collar or otherwise tries to remove it. This is normal, and the dog should not be punished for it. It is best to simply ignore the dog and allow him to work out his own issues with the collar.

The dog should be allowed to wear the collar 24 hours a day for a number of days to get used to the feel of the collar on his neck. After the dog is accepting the collar well, it is time to start introducing the leash. A lightweight leash works best for this process.

Simply attach the leash to the puppy's collar and allow him to walk around the house with it. The dog should of course be supervised during this process in order to make sure he does not get the leash caught on anything. Getting the leash caught or snagged could frighten the puppy and create a leash phobia that will be hard to overcome.

In the beginning, the leash should only be attached for a few minutes at a time. It is important to attach the leash at happy times, such as playtime, meal time, etc. It is important for the dog to associate the leash with happy things. When the leash is not attached to the puppy, it is a good idea to keep it near the dog's food and water bowls. The puppy should be encouraged to investigate the leash, and to discover that it is not something to fear.

After the puppy is used to walking around with the leash attached, take the end of the leash in your hand and just hold it. Allow him to walk around. If the puppy bumps into the end of the leash, just allow him to react and move as he desires. The goal of this exercise is to simply allow him to get used to the feel of the collar and the leash.

It usually takes new users a little while to get used to using the training collar, and some styles of training collar require more finesse than others.

If you are unsure which collar to choose, be sure to ask a

professional dog trainer, or the management staff at your local pet store, for help.

The use of choke collars is strongly discouraged for puppies. They are cruel corrective means that can   damage their neck´s delicate skeletal structure.

ACCEPTING THE COLLAR AND LEASH

Learning to walk on a collar and leash is the basis of all further training for every dog, especially if he is a puppy. Until the dog has learned to accept the collar and leash, it will be impossible to perform any additional training.

It is important to allow the puppy plenty of time to get used to wearing the collar and leash before ever attempting to lead him.

It is best to perform this exercise in the home or other environment where the puppy feels safe and secure. After the puppy is comfortable and content walking on the leash in the home, it can slowly be taken outside. It is best to make these outside trips very short at the beginning, and to lengthen them slowly over time. Some puppies take to the collar and leash immediately, while others may require some additional time.

Walking on a collar and lead is an important skill that every puppy must learn.

Even the best trained dog should never be taken outside the

home or yard without a sturdy collar and leash.

Even if your puppy is trained perfectly to go off lead, accidents and distractions do happen, and a collar, with proper identification attached, is the best way to be sure you will get your beloved companion back.

Of course before you can teach your new puppy to accept a leash, he or she must first learn to accept wearing a collar.

The first step is to choose a collar that fits the dog properly.

It is important to measure the puppy's neck, and to choose a collar size accordingly. After the collar has been put on the puppy, simply let him or her get used to it. It is not unusual for a puppy to try to pull on the collar, whine, roll or squirm when first introduced to a collar.

The best strategy is to simply ignore the puppy and let him or her get used to the collar.

It is a mistake to either punish the puppy for playing with the collar or to encourage the behavior.

Distracting the puppy often helps, and playing with a favorite toy, or eating some favorite treats, can help the puppy quickly forget that he or she is wearing this strange piece of equipment.

After the puppy has learned to accept the collar, try adding the leash.

Hook the leash to the collar and simply sit and watch the puppy.

Obviously, this should only be done either in the house or in a confined outdoor area. The puppy should be allowed to drag the leash around on its own, but of course the owner should keep a close eye on the puppy to ensure that the leash does not become snagged or hung up on anything.

At first, the leash should only be left on for a few minutes at a time. It is a good idea to attach the leash at mealtimes, playtime and other positive times in the life of the puppy.

That way the puppy will begin to associate the leash with good things and look forward to it. If the puppy shows a high degree of fear of the leash, it is a good idea to place it next to the food bowl for a while to let him get used to it slowly.

Eventually, he will come to understand that the leash is nothing to be afraid of.

After the puppy is comfortable with walking around the house wearing the leash, it is time for you to pick up the end of the leash for a few minutes.

You should not try to walk the puppy on the leash; simply hold the end of the leash and follow the puppy around as he or she walks around.

You should try to avoid situations where the leash becomes taut and any pulling or straining on the leash should be avoided. It is fine for the puppy to sit down.

Try a few games with the collar and lead.

For instance, back up and encourage the puppy to walk toward you.

Don't drag the puppy forward, simply encourage him to come to you.

If he does, praise him profusely and reward him with a food treat or toy.

You should always strive to make all the time spent on the leash as pleasant as possible.

It is important to give the puppy plenty of practice in getting used to walking on the leash in the home. It is best to do plenty of work in the home, since it is a safe environment with few distractions.

After the puppy is comfortable walking indoors on a leash, it is time to start going outside, beginning of course in a small, enclosed area like a fenced yard.

Once he has mastered walking calmly outdoors on a leash, it is time to visit some places where there are more distractions.

You may want to start with a place like a neighbor's yard.

Walking your new puppy around the neighborhood is a good way to introduce your neighbors to the new puppy, while giving the puppy valuable experience in avoiding distractions and focusing on his leash training.

Puppies sometimes develop bad habits with their leashes, such as biting or chewing on the leash. To discourage this type of behavior, try applying a little bit of bitter apple, Tabasco sauce or similar substance (just make sure the substance you use is not toxic to dogs). This strategy usually convinces puppies that chewing the leash is a bad idea.

NO PULLING ON THE LEASH

Pulling on the leash is one of the most common misbehaviors seen on all kinds of dogs.

Puppies and adult dogs alike can often be seen taking their owners for walks, instead of the other way around. Pulling on the leash can be much more than an annoying habit. Leash pulling can lead to escape in the case of a break in the collar or leash, and an out of control, off leash dog can be both destructive and dangerous to itself and to others.

Leash pulling can result from a variety of different things. In some cases, the puppy may simply be so excited to go for a walk that he or she is unable to control themselves. In other cases, the dog sees itself as the leader of the pack, and he or she simply takes the "leadership position" at the front of the pack.

If excitement is the motivation for leash pulling, simply giving the puppy a few minutes to calm down can often be a big help. Simply stand with the dog on the leash for a couple minutes and let the initial excitement of the upcoming walk pass. After the initial excitement has worn off, many dogs are willing to walk calmly on their leash.

If the problem is one of control, however, some retraining may be in order. All puppy training starts with the owner establishing him or herself as the alpha dog, or pack leader, and without this basic respect and understanding, no effective training can occur.

For dogs exhibiting these type of control issues, a step back to basic obedience commands is in order. These dogs can often be helped through a formal obedience school structure. The dog trainer will of course be sure to train the handler as well as the dog, and any good dog trainer will insist on working with the dog owner as well as the dog.

The basis of teaching your puppy to walk calmly on the lead is teaching it to calmly accept the collar and lead.

A puppy that is bouncing up and down while the collar is being put on will not walk properly.

*Begin by asking your puppy to sit down, and insisting that he sit still while the collar is put on. If the dog begins to get up, or gets up on his own after the collar is on, be sure to sit him back down immediately.

*Only begin the walk after the puppy has sat calmly to have the collar put on, and continued to sit calmly as the leash is attached.

*Once the leash is attached, it is important to make the puppy walk calmly toward the door.

*If the puppy jumps or surges ahead, gently correct him with a tug of the leash and return him to a sitting position.

*Make the puppy stay and then move on again.

*Repeat this process until the puppy is walking calmly by your side.

*Repeat the above process when you reach the door. The puppy should not be allowed to surge out of the door, or to pull you through the open door.

*If the puppy begins this behavior, return him to the house and make him sit quietly until he can be trusted to walk through the door properly. Starting the walk in control is vital to creating a well-mannered dog.

As you begin your walk, it is vital to keep the attention of the puppy focused on you at all times.

Remember, the puppy should look to you for guidance, not take the lead himself.

When walking, it is important to stop often. Every time you stop, your puppy should stop. Getting into the habit of asking your puppy to sit down every time you stop is a good way to keep your puppy's attention focused on you.

Make sure your puppy is looking at you, then move off again. If the dog begins to surge ahead, immediately stop and ask the puppy to sit.

Repeat this process until the puppy is reliability staying at your side. Each time the dog does what you ask him to, be sure to reward him with a treat, a toy or just your praise.

Remember that if your puppy pulls on the leash and you continue to walk him anyway, you are inadvertently rewarding that unwanted behavior.

Dogs learn whether you are teaching them or not, and learning the wrong things now will make learning the right things later that much harder.

It is important to be consistent in your expectations.

Every time the puppy begins to pull ahead, immediately stop

and make the dog sit. Continue to have the puppy sit quietly until his focus is solely on you. Then start out again, making sure to immediately stop moving if the dog surges ahead.

LESSON SIXTEEN

LEASH WALKING YOUR PUPPY

TEACHING A PUPPY TO WALK on a leash is not always an easy task. It is in the dog's nature to want to wander off and sniff everything that comes in his path. However, this behavior is not conducive to a pleasant and athletic walk. You, his master, have to strike the balance between allowing him to explore his world and walking in a controlled way.

The first thing you will need to do is purchase an appropriate leash for your dog.

Make sure that it is the right weight according to how much your puppy weighs right now. Even if he will eventually be 75 pounds, he will not be able to handle a heavy leash while he is still small.

The next thing to choose is a collar for walking. Some people use harnesses are leaders that attach around his head and snout. Both of these products can help you better control your puppy in a humane and safe way.

Choker collars are not recommended for any breed of dog, as there is significant danger of hurting the animal. If your puppy is small a simple collar and your leash might be plenty.

However, you will want to use the same type of device, like a harness or leader, which you will use when he is bigger.

One of the important steps to ensuring that your walk is pleasant is to try to get your puppy to do his 'number two' business before you leave your home. If he learns that the walk is the time to go to the potty then you will almost always be stuck carrying around a bag of his waste on your walks.

He should learn to potty in a specified spot in your yard. Of course, to be on the safe side you should always carry a bag with you for picking up any potential dog droppings.

The part of the training process is time consuming and requires a great deal of patience. Do not expect your first walk to be a long one, distance wise at least. Think of it as a training session that requires lots of stopping and starting to get it right.

LEASH WALKING FACTS

*You should always walk your puppy at least twice a day, if not more while he is young. This will help him get used to walking and allow him to burn energy.

*Choose a side that you want your dog to walk on. He should always walk on the side that you choose, either right or left, Keep in mind that this behavior will stay with him so make sure that you are comfortable with the position of the leash and your arms.

*Take a few steps with your dog, when he begins to pull stop and make him sit. Reward him with praise for sitting and then start again.

*Each time he begins to pull on the leash, repeat the stop and sit pattern. *This might mean you only manage to take a few steps before you have to stop and begin again.

*Allow your dog to veer off the path, as long as he does not pull and smell things. He or she will also occasionally mark with their urine, this is normal behavior, allow them to do it as long as it does not become constant.

*When your dog stays with you, at your side and keeping pace reward him with praise and a treat. Remember he wants to please you; he just has to be taught how to do that.

*When you come upon other people or dogs your puppy may experience anxiety, which will cause him to pull or bark. Reassure him with affection that he is ok and that you are there with him. If he gets too excited have him sit and wait for people to pass.

*Children are always especially interested in puppies and it is in your best interest to teach your dog how to interact with them. But, you have to be in control of the situation. If you are comfortable with it you may allow others to pet your dog, but make him sit and behave while they do it.

*As your dog gets older you may consider allowing him to walk off leash. Do this with great care, especially when cars are around. Even the most well trained dog is still an animal and as such, is unpredictable. You would not want anything bad to happen to your dog because he was off leash in an unsafe area.

WALKING ON A LEAD

After you have become familiar with the way the training collar works, it is time to begin using it to train your puppy to walk properly on a lead.

As Cesar says, a well trained dog will walk at his owner's side on a loose lead, neither dropping behind nor charging ahead. The well trained dog will also vary his pace to meet that of his handler. Under no circumstances should the handler be forced to change his or her pace to match that of the dog.

If the puppy does begin to charge ahead, it is important to correct the dog promptly by giving a quick tug on the leash. This will give the puppy a good reminder that he needs to change his pace.

It is important to quickly relieve the pressure as soon as the puppy responds. The training collar is designed to relieve pressure as soon as the leash is loosened.

Most puppys will immediately respond to corrections by a good, properly used training collar.

If the puppy does not respond as directed, it may be necessary to apply greater pressure. This can be especially true of large dogs or those who have preexisting behavior or control problems.

If you are still unable to get a response from your puppy, it is possible that you are using a training collar that is not large enough for your dog.

If you think this may be the case, be sure to ask for expert advice before proceeding.

DOG TRAINING OFF LEASH

Many dog owners are anxious to give their four legged companions the freedom of going off leash, but it is important not to rush that important step. Dogs should only be allowed off their leash after they have become masters of all the basic obedience commands, such as walking at your heel, sitting and staying on command

Another skill that must be completely mastered before the puppy can be taken off the leash is the come when called command. Even if the puppy can heel, sit and stay perfectly, if he cannot be relied upon to come when called, he is not ready to be taken off the leash.

Taking any puppy off the leash, especially in a busy, crowded area, or one with a lot of traffic, is a big step and not one to be taken lightly. It is vital to adequately test your puppy in a safe environment before taking him off his leash. After all, the leash is the main instrument of control.

You must be absolutely certain you can rely on your voice

commands for control before removing the leash.

After the puppy has been trained to understand the sit, stay and come when called commands, it is important to challenge the puppy with various distractions.

It is a good idea to start by introducing other people, other animals, or both, while the puppy is in a safe environment like a fenced in yard. Have a friend or neighbor stand just outside the fence while you hold your puppy on the leash.

As the friend or family member walks around the outside of the fence, watch your dog's reactions closely.

If he starts to pull at the leash, quickly tug him back.

Repeat this exercise until the puppy will reliably remain at your side.

After this, you can try dropping the leash, and eventually removing the leash and repeating the distraction.

It is important to vary the distractions, such as introducing other animals, other people, traffic, rolling balls, etc.

After your puppy is able to remain still in the face of distraction, start introducing the come when called lessons with distractions in place.

Try to invite some of the neighbors, and their dogs over to play with each other. As the dogs are playing in the fenced in yard, try calling your puppy. When the puppy comes to you, immediately give him lots of praise, and perhaps a food reward.

Once the puppy has been rewarded, immediately allow him to go back to playing. Repeat this several times throughout the day, making sure each time to reward the puppy and immediately allow him to go back to his fun.

After the puppy has seemingly mastered coming when called in his own yard, try finding a local dog park or similar area where you can practice with your puppy. It is important to make the area small, or to choose a fenced in area, in case you lose control of the dog.

If you cannot find a fenced in area, choose an area well away from people and cars.

Practice with your puppy by allowing him to play with other dogs, or just to sniff around, then calling your puppy.

When he comes to you, immediately reward and praise him, then let him resume his previous activities.

Doing this will teach the dog that coming to you is the best option and the one most likely to bring both rewards and continued good times.

Only after the dog has consistently demonstrated the ability to come when called, even when there are many distractions around, is it safe to allow him time off leash.

Off leash time should never be unsupervised time.

It is important, both for your well-being and your puppy's, which you know where, he is and what he is doing at all times.

It is easy for a dog to get into trouble quickly, so you should always keep an eye on him, whether he is chasing squirrels in the park, playing with other dogs, or just chasing a ball with the neighbor's kids.

A PROPERLY FITTED COLLAR

Determining if the training collar is the right size is relatively easy. The ideal size training collar should fit snugly, yet comfortably over the dog's head. It is important that the training collar not fit too tightly, but it should not be too loose either.

A training collar that is too tight will be too hard to put on and off. On the other hand, a training collar that is too loose can accidentally fall off of the dog's head when it lowers its head.

It is also important to know that a training collar that is too long for the dog requires a great deal of finesse to use properly. A collar that is too long can still be used, but it will require more skill on the part of the handler.

It is best to measure the dog's neck with a tape measure, and then add 2 to 3 inches to that measurement. So if your dog has a neck 12" in diameter, you would want to buy a training collar that is 14" in length. Chain slip collars are generally sized in two inch increments.

When fitting a training collar, the part of the chain which is connected to the leash should be on the top of the dog's neck. With this type of arrangement, the collar releases the instant the leash is loosened. Training collars work by making the collar tight and loose in a fast manner. Tightening the collar is the first part of the correction, and making it loose is the second part of the correction.

If the part of the training collar that is attached to the leash is not on the top of the dog's neck, the collar can still be made tight, but it will not release back to a loose state easily.

This constant pressure on the dog's neck initiates a counter response on the part of the animal, and the dog will quickly learn to pull and strain against the leash.

Finally, it is important to purchase a training collar that is well made and strong. Buying a high quality training collar, slip collar or choke collar is vital to the safety of yourself and your dog.

If the worst happens, and your puppy's training collar does break, it is important not to panic. Most dogs will be unaware that they have broken the collar, at least for a few minutes. In most cases, if you act as if the leash is still connected, you can probably get control of your dog back quickly.

When securing a loose dog, the best strategy is to make a quick slip lead by running the snap on the leash through its handle and then slipping it over the dog's head. It may not be the best arrangement, but it will certainly do in a pinch.

LESSON SEVENTEEN

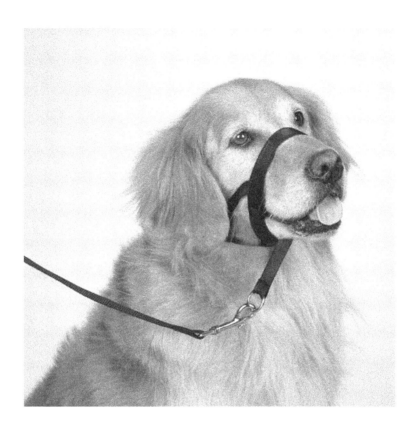

HEAD COLLAR TRAINING

THE HEAD COLLAR has become an increasingly popular dog training tool in the past several years.

Two of the most well-known brands of head collar on the market are the Gentle Leader and the Halti, but there are many other brands that incorporate the basic head collar concept.

Many people find the Gentle Leader easier to fit that the Halti, and in addition the Gentle Leader is designed to fasten around the dog's neck.

The advantage of this design is that even if the dog is somehow able to wriggle out of the muzzle, it is still wearing a collar. This safety feature is very important, especially during training outside or in novel situations.

On the other hand, the Halti offers better control of the dog, and for this reason it is often favored when working with very aggressive dogs.

 Training a dog with a head collar has a number of advantages over training with a traditional or training collar. For one thing, head collars are often easier to use for beginning dog trainers than are training collars.

Head collars are also quite effective at preventing dogs from pulling, or controlling and retraining dogs that tend to pull.

Head collars can also be quite effective at controlling dogs in difficult situations, such as controlling a dog that wants to be with other dogs. Most owners know of some situations in which their dogs are difficult to control, and head collars can be quite effective at controlling these volatile situations.

Head collars can be excellent for controlling dogs that are very strong, or for working with a dog in an area that contains a great many distractions. For instance, head collars are great for when your puppy is on an outing, or in an area where there will be other dogs and other distractions.

Even though a head collar can be a great tool, it should not be used as a replacement for effective dog training. A head collar is most effective when it is used in combination with strong and sensible dog training methods, such as reward training and other forms of positive reinforcement.

DISADVANTAGES OF HEAD COLLARS

Even though head collars have many advantages, they have some distinct disadvantages as well. For one thing, head collars tend to make many dogs dependent on the equipment, and they quickly learn the difference between their regular collar and the head collar, and adjust their behavior accordingly.

In addition, some dogs, particularly those not accustomed to wearing a head collar, dislike wearing it and paw at it, try to rub it off or pull excessively. If your dog exhibits this behavior, the best strategy is to keep it moving until it learns to accept the collar.

A good alternative is to have the dog sit by pulling up on the dog's head.

Another disadvantage of the head collar is the reaction that many people have to it. Many people think that a head collar is a muzzle, and react to the dog as if it may bite. While this is not necessarily a defect of the head collar, many people do find it troublesome.

Dog training with a head collar is much like training with a training collar or any other equipment. While the head collar can be an important and useful tool, it is important to use it appropriately, follow all package instructions, and to combine its use with solid training methods.

The eventual goal of dog training with a head collar should be to have the dog behave as well with a regular collar as it does with the specialized head collar.

LESSON EIGHTEEN

CRATE TRAINING YOUR PUPPY

AS YOU ARE HOUSEBREAKING your puppy you will also be training him to stay in a crate or kennel.

A lot of people think the kennel is a punishment for a poorly behaved dog, but that is not at all the case.

The crate is your puppy's very own space!

He will enjoy it and probably spend time in the crate even when the door is open.

Training your puppy to stay in a crate when you are not home or are asleep saves a great deal of anxiety for both you and your new pet.

As stated before, dogs are den dwelling animals. The feel of a small space is comforting to them. You may even want to cover a wire cage so that he feels even mor e secure inside it.

Dogs also have no sense of time. That is why they are always excited to see you, whether you have been gone ten minutes or ten hours.

When they are in the crate all they will do is sleep.

When you are not home and they are out of the crate they will either sleep or get into trouble. Putting the puppy in a crate saves them from getting into trouble.

Crate training your dog is also a great step in avoiding unwanted behaviors like digging in garbage cans, chewing on non-toys, and climbing on furniture. It also protects him from getting in a dangerous situation in your home.

Dogs will eat things they are not supposed to eat or get trapped in small places very easily. Puppies are in even greater danger because of their small size and lack of depth perception, so a crate is really a safety precaution.

There are two standard types of dog crates, the wire mesh ones and the plastic kind. Both are good choices for your dog.

If you plan to travel by plane with your puppy you might want to invest in an airline approved crate, which typically is the plastic kind.

The wire mesh ones are collapsible which makes them easy to move and to clean.

GETTING YOR DOG INSIDE THE CRATE

When you first bring the puppy home he might not readily go into the crate. Make it appealing by placing treats or toys inside.

Again, use a simple command like "Inside" or "Kennel" repeatedly until your dog goes in the kennel.

A technique used by Cesar consists in placing doggie treats inside the crate and having the dog entering on its own.

In any case, once your puppy is inside the crate make sure to reward him with praise and a treat.

You will be surprised to find that after a while you will not even need to give him treats or say the command. He will pick up and go into the kennel on his own.

Do not be alarmed if your puppy whines a little bit when he is inside the kennel. It is not because he wants out, rather because he wants you inside with him.

Dogs crave your constant attention, but he needs to learn to be comfortable by himself and in his own space.

You might go over and offer him a few comforting words, but do not sit nervously by him or let him out when he behaves this way. Doing that will only enforce the whining and he will train you instead of you training him.

Some people choose to place a dog bed or blanket inside the kennel to make him more comfortable.

As your dog gets older and larger he might not need the blanket, especially if you live in a hot climate. But, while he is a puppy it is a great comfort item. You might even put in a piece of clothing that smells like you to give him more comfort. Some people recommend keeping water in the kennel or feeding the puppy in it.

The choice is up to you, but be aware that both of these have the potential to create quite a big mess.

One of the best ways to make sure your puppy is comfortable is to keep him near you.

The kennel should be strategically placed in an area that the family hangs out in most of the time.

The family room is a good choice as opposed to a bedroom that is often empty. Having the kennel in the family room will encourage your puppy to sit in there while the rest of you are watching television or having other family time.

If you do not like the look of a kennel consider dressing it up so that it fits with your decor better. You can easily cut a piece of wood to fit the top of it and then place a tablecloth or other fabric over it. Then it simply looks like an end table and not a dog kennel in your living room.

A puppy should never be in the kennel for more then eight hours at a time.

If this means that you have to come home at lunch or wake up during the night to let the dog out, then you must do those things.

Think about that time commitment before you bring the dog home.

Also, the kennel should never be a place of punishment.

When your dog is put in the kennel he should go in happily, knowing that you will be back and that he is not in trouble.

CRATE TRAINING BASICS

Crate training is one of the most effective ways of house breaking any puppy or dog. It training is very efficient, and very effective, since it uses the natural instinct of the dog to achieve the desired result of a clean house and a well-trained puppy.

The concept behind crate training is that a dog naturally strives to avoid soiling the area where it eats and sleeps. By placing the puppy in the crate, this instinct is enhanced. The dog will come to see the crate as its den, and it will try to avoid soiling its den.

The key to successful crate training for a puppy or an older dog, as with other forms of dog training, is to establish a good routine.

This routine will enhance the ability of the dog to do its business in the right place, and avoid eliminating in the wrong place.

It is important to shower the dog with praise each and every time it eliminates in the established potty area, and not to express frustration or anger when the dog makes a mistake.

It is important to confine the dog or puppy to a small part of the house, generally one puppy proofed room, when you are not at home.

The room should contain a soft bed, fresh water and some favorite toys to prevent the dog from becoming bored and frustrated.

Crate training is different from confining the dog to one room, however.

With crate training, the puppy or dog is confined to a crate when unsupervised. The idea is that the dog will think of this crate as its home, and not want to soil is home.

When crate training, it is important to remove the dog from the crate as soon as possible after returning home, and to take the dog promptly to the previously established potty area. When the dog does its business in this toilet area, be sure to provide lots of praise and treats. It is important that the dog learn to associate proper toilet procedures with good things like treats and toys.

It is important to never leave the dog in its crate for long periods of time, as this will confuse the dog and force it to soil its sleeping area. The crate is simply a tool, and it should not be abused by leaving the dog in it for extended periods of time. If the dog is left in the crate for too long, it could set back the training program by weeks if not months.

The dog should only be confined to the crate when you are at home. During day time except during the night time, dog should be given the opportunity to relieve itself every 45 minutes or so. Each time the dog is taken out; it should be put on a leash and immediately taken outside. Once outside the house, the dog should be given three to five minutes to do its business. If the dog does not eliminate in this time period, it should be immediately returned to the crate.

If the puppy does its business during the set time period, it should be rewarded with praise, food, play, affection and either an extended walk or a period of play inside or outside the home.

During the crate training period, it is important to keep a daily diary of when the dog does its business each day. If the dog is on a regular feeding schedule, the potty schedule should be consistent as well. Having a good idea of when the dog needs to eliminate each day will be a big help during the house training process. After the dog has used his established potty area, you will be able to give the dog free run of the house to play and enjoy him.

It is very important to not punish the puppy or dog when it makes a mistake or has an accident during the crate training process.

If there's been an accident, simply clean it up.

Accidents during house training mean that you have provided the dog with unsupervised access to the house too quickly.

The dog should not be allowed unsupervised access to the home until you can trust her bowel and bladder habits.

If mistakes do occur, it is best to go back to crate training.

Taking a couple of steps back will help move the house training process along, while moving too quickly could set things back.

CRATE TRAINING: THINGS TO REMEMBER

According to the American dog trainer Daniel Stevens, author of the Secrets to Dog Training guide to dog obedience training and founder of the Kingdom of Pets dog training network, a puppy is unlikely to soil his own rest and play area. So the crate is a good way to teach him to hold it in until you take him to the designated area to do his business.

This will teach him control of his bodily functions and reinforce the fact that he should only do his business in the designated place. Once this has happened, you could find that he starts to do this more and more and it may become a hard habit to break.

Daniel Stevens also explains that dog owners need to realize that "CONFINEMENT" doesn't mean the same thing to you as it does to your puppy. Their very own crate is the one place a dog can go where they know they don't have to DO anything, such as protect or alert or even keep you company. In the crate, they really don't have to make any decisions at all... and for them, that's a HUGE relief.

Crate training is an effective method used by many dog owners to house train any dog as well as keep them safe from the potential dangers around the house. Your puppy should be actively encouraged to think of his crate as a safe area –somewhere that he can go to get some rest or some peace and quiet.

Make the crate as comfortable as possible for your puppy, putting in some toys and soft bedding to put him at ease.

According to Daniel Stevens these are the things to remember when crate training your puppy:

Don't force it: Never try and rush crate training, otherwise you will make things more difficult for you and your pet. It can take your puppy a while to get used to it, and you should be patient and understanding with him.

Monitor the time: The crate is not meant to be a place where your puppy spends all of his time. It is not a substitute for responsible dog care or your warm companionship. Having a dog is pointless if you are going to put him in a crate all day while you work, all evening while you have dinner and get the house tidied, and all night while you sleep. The crate should be used as and when you need it, not as a permanent measure to keep the dog from under your feet.

Careful with puppies: When you are using the crate for your puppy, remember that she will need to relieve herself quite often. You should let her out and take her to her designated area around once hourly to avoid accidents inside the crate.

No collars: Make sure that you take his collar off before you put him in the crate, otherwise you may cause a choking hazard.

Make it comfortable: Your puppy should see the crate as a safe area – a place of their own. Therefore, aim to make it as comfortable as possible, with toys, blankets, and anything else that will make the dog feel more at home. In addition, remember your puppy always needs access to fresh water so make sure that this is provided.

Do not use it as punishment: Your puppy should never be sent to her crate as a form of punishment. Similarly, you should make sure that he cannot be harassed by anyone while he is in his crate. Remember you want her crate to seem like her safe haven.

Do not use a second-hand one: You will have a much better chance of getting your puppy to successfully use a crate if it is brand new. A secondhand crate will carry the residual smell of its previous occupier, which your puppy will probably not like.

LESSON NINETEEN

BARKING AND YOUR PUPPY

DOGS LIKE TO BARK, it makes them feel powerful and in control of their surroundings. However, barking can be a nuisance that you need to control in order to keep a happy dog and household.

By training your dog to 'speak' on command he will be less likely to do it without being instructed to do so (see my previous book *DOG TRICKS THE PACK LEADER'S WAY*).

Barking is your dogs´ warning system, so when he barks when he wants in or to warn you, praise him for one bark.

This should teach him that barking once gets your affection but barking excessively only gets him ignored.

Dogs should not be left outside unattended.

While a lot of people see nothing wrong with leaving a dog in a fenced yard while they are at work or away from the house, it is not the best choice for your dog.

Your domesticated dog needs you, when you are not around he will feel anxious which will cause him to bark excessively.

He might even exhibit other behaviors like digging or finding ways to escape your yard. A dog that is comfortable and loved is not left outside unattended.

One of the easy ways to manage your dogs barking is to understand why he does it.

Many people experience the problem of their dog barking whenever someone walks by the front window of their home. Dogs do this because they are territorial, when they bark at people walking by their intention is to scare them away.

Any person who is just walking by your house will continue their walk because; obviously they are not scared of a dog that is inside the house.

Your dog does not understand this concept.

He thinks that because the person continued to walk, that he must have scared them away. This enforces his idea that the barking works, so he will continue to do it.

The best way to manage this behavior is to teach your puppy that his barking, in fact, does not work.

You will need to enlist the help of some friends who are not familiar with your dog to teach him not to bark. Have those people walk by your house when the dog is looking.

When he starts barking they should stop and continue standing in front of your house. The dog will quickly realize that his barking did not work, but also that someone on the sidewalk is not a threat.

Training a dog not to bark can be tricky, since dogs are also a good warning system should someone come into our home uninvited.

There is a fine line between teaching your dog to behave and still allowing him to be protective of you and your home. When the puppy exhibits behaviors that are meant to protect you and your family, or his pack, reward him with praise. He should learn the difference between this and unwanted behavior fairly quickly.

LESSON TWENTY

PROBLEM BEHAVIORS

THERE ARE MANY REASONS for teaching proper dog behavior, and teaching such behavior has many benefits for both the human and canine partners. Dog behavior training is vital to such life and death issues as preventing aggression, controlling dog on dog aggression problems and teaching dogs to interact properly with both their handlers and with other members of the family.

Understanding how dogs evolved, and how dogs interact with each other, is very important to understanding how to properly train your puppy to be a devoted, loyal companion.

The original dogs were probably orphaned wolf pups adopted by early humans. These wild dogs probably learned to perform behaviors that their human protectors valued, such as guarding the cave or scaring off predators. In exchange for these valued behaviors, the humans probably provided their new companions with foods, protection and shelter.

That kind of relationship still exists today, of course, and dogs still can, and do, perform valuable jobs for their human benefactors. Those jobs include herding and guarding livestock, guarding property, guarding people, and finding game.

When planning a dog training program, it is important to know that dogs are pack animals. In wild dog societies, packs are formed, and each member of the pack quickly learns his or her place in the pecking order. Except in the event of death or injury to the alpha dog, the hierarchy never changes once it has been established. The lower dogs know not to challenge the alpha dog, and the alpha dog understand his place as leader of the pack.

All the other dogs in the pack look to the alpha dog for leadership, in important survival issues like finding food and avoiding larger predators. In order to properly train your dog and gain its respect, it is important for you to become the alpha dog.

That is because a dog that sees its owner as a superior leader will follow the commands the owner gives without question. Getting the respect of the dog is the most important step to proper dog training, and it will form the basis of all subsequent training.

The reasons for training a dog properly are many, especially in today's world.

A well-mannered, obedient dog is a joy to be around, both for the owner and his or her family, and for people in the community at large.

In addition, seeing a well-mannered dog sets people's mind at ease, especially with breeds of dog thought to be dangerous, such as Dobermans, rottweilers and pit bulls.

When training dogs and dealing with unwanted dog behaviors, it is important to understand the motivating factors behind those behaviors. For example, many dogs exhibit unwanted behaviors such as chewing and destroying furniture due to separation anxiety.

Dealing with the sources of problem behaviors is an important first step toward eliminating those problem behaviors.

Many dogs exhibit unwanted behaviors as a result of stress in the animal's life, and its inability to cope with that stress. The goal of a good dog training program is to allow the dog to tolerate greater levels of stress without becoming a problem animal.

When dealing with dog behavior, it is important not to confuse human behavior with dog behavior. While there is a great temptation on the part of dog owners to see their dogs as almost human, in reality dogs and humans have very different motivations, and very different reactions to similar situations.

One trait that humans and dogs do share, however, is the need to form close social groups and strong bonds within those social groups. This bonding is important to both humans and dogs, but it has served vastly different ends as both species have evolved and changed over time.

ELIMINATING BITING BEHAVIORS

Bringing home a new puppy is always an exciting time. Introducing the new puppy to the family should be fun for both yourself and your puppy. One of the first challenges, however, to the excitement of the new puppy, is curbing inappropriate puppy behaviors.

Biting and mouthing is a common activity for many young puppies and dogs. Puppies naturally bite and mouth each other when playing with siblings, and they extend this behavior to their human companions. While other puppies have thick skin, however, humans do not, so it is important to teach your puppy what is appropriate, and what is not, when it comes to using those sharp teeth.

The first part of training the puppy is to inhibit the biting reflex. Biting might be cute and harmless with a 5 pound puppy, but it is neither cute nor harmless when that dog has grown to adulthood. Therefore, puppies should be taught to control their bit before they reach the age of four months. Puppies normally learn to inhibit their bite from their mothers and their littermates, but since they are taken away from their mothers so young, many never learn this important lesson. It is therefore up to the humans in the puppy's life to teach this lesson.

One great way to inhibit the biting reflex is to allow the puppy to play and socialize with other puppies and socialized older dogs. Puppies love to tumble, roll and play with each other, and when puppies play they bite each other constantly. This is the best way for puppies to learn to control themselves when they bite. If one puppy becomes too rough when playing, the rest of the group will punish him for that inappropriate behavior. Through this type of socialization, the puppy will learn to control his biting reflex.

Proper socialization has other benefits as well, including teaching the dog to not be fearful of other dogs, and to work off their excess energy. Puppies that are allowed to play with other puppies learn important socialization skills generally learn to become better members of their human family. Puppies that get less socialization can be more destructive, more hyperactive and exhibit other problem behaviors.

In addition, lack of socialization in puppies often causes fearful and aggressive behaviors to develop. Dogs often react aggressively to new situations, especially if they are not properly socialized. In order for a dog to become a member of the community as well as the household, it should be socialized to other people, especially children. Dogs make a distinction between their owners and other people, and between children and adults. It is important, therefore, to introduce the puppy to both children and adults.

The best time to socialize a puppy to young children is when it is still very young, generally when it is four months old or younger. One reason for this is that mothers of young children may be understandably reluctant to allow their children to approach large dogs or older puppies. This is especially true with large breed dogs, or with breeds of dogs that have a reputation for aggressive behavior.

Teaching your puppy to trust and respect you is a very effective way to prevent biting. Gaining the trust and respect of your puppy is the basis for all dog training, and for correcting problem behaviors.

It is important to never hit or slap the puppy, either during training or any other time. Physical punishment is the surest way to erode the trust and respect that must form the basis of an effective training program.

Reprimanding a dog will not stop him from biting – it will simply scare and confuse him.

Training a puppy not to bite is a vital part of any puppy training program. Biting behaviors that are not corrected will only get worse, and what seemed like harmless behavior in a puppy can quickly escalate to dangerous, destructive behavior in an adult dog.

WHINING, HOWLING AND BARKING

Let's start with one of the most frequently encountered problem behaviors in both dogs and puppies. While some barking and other vocalizing is perfectly normal, in many cases barking, howling and whining can become problematic. This is particularly important for those living in apartment buildings, or in closely spaced homes. Fielding complaints about barking is not the best way for you and your puppy to meet the neighbors.

Some tips of dealing with excessive whining, barking and howling include:

*If your puppy or dog is howling or whining while confined to its crate, immediately take it to its toilet area. Most puppies and dogs will whine when they need to do their business.

*It is important to teach a dog or a puppy to accept being alone. Many dogs suffer from separation anxiety, and these stressed dogs can exhibit all sorts of destructive and annoying behaviors. It is important to accustom the puppy to being left on its own, even when the owner is at home.

*Always strive to make the puppy or dog as comfortable as possible. Always attend to the physical and psychological needs of the dog by providing food, water and toys.

*If the dog is whining, check for obvious reasons first. Is the water dish empty? Is the dog showing signs of illness? Has his or her favorite toy rolled under the furniture? Is the temperature of the room too hot or too cold?

*Do not reward the puppy or dog for whining. If the dog whines when left alone, for instance, it would be a mistake to go to the dog every time it whines.

*After you have ensured that the dog's physical needs are being met, and that discomfort is not responsible for the whining, do not hesitate to reprimand the dog for inappropriate behavior.

PROBLEM CHEWING

Puppies naturally chew, and they tend to explore their world using their mouths and teeth. While chewing may be normal, however, it is not acceptable, and it is important to nip any chewing problems in the bud to prevent the chewing puppy from growing into a chewing dog.

Providing a variety of chew toys is important when teaching a puppy what is appropriate to chew and what is not. Providing a variety of attractive chew toys is a good way to keep the puppy entertained and to keep his teeth and gums exercised. Scented or flavored toys are great choices for most puppies.

The puppy should be encouraged to play with these chosen toys, and the puppy should be effusively praised every time he or she plays with or chews these toys.

Another great strategy is to encourage the puppy to get a toy every time he or she greets you. Every time the puppy greets you or a member of your family, teach him to get one of his toys.

It is also important to exercise good housekeeping techniques when training a puppy not to chew on inappropriate items. Keeping the area to which the puppy has access free and clean is important. Keeping items out of reach of the puppy will go a long way toward discouraging inappropriate chewing. Try to keep the puppy's area free of shoes, trash, and other items, and always make sure that the area has been properly puppy proofed.

If the puppy does pick up an inappropriate item like a shoe, distract the puppy and quickly replace the item with one of its toys!

Also, after the puppy has taken the toy, praise it for playing with and chewing that toy!

Try booby trapping items the dog should avoid by spraying them with bitter apple, Tabasco sauce or other nasty but non-toxic items!

ELIMINATING BAD HABITS

Anyone who owns a dog or puppy will eventually run into the need to eliminate unwanted habits.

While most dogs are eager to please their owners and smart enough to do what is asked of them, it is important for the owner to properly communicate just what constitutes acceptable and unacceptable behaviors.

Each type of unacceptable behavior requires its own specific cures, and in most cases the cures will need to be tailored to fit the specific personality of the dog.

Every breed of dog has its own unique personality characteristics, and every individual within that breed has his or her own unique personality.

OTHER PROBLEM BEHAVIORS

Other canine problem behaviors include:

Problem #1 – Jumping up on people

One of the most frequently cited problems with dogs is that of jumping up on people.

Unfortunately, this is one of those behaviors that are often inadvertently encouraged by well- meaning owners. After all, it is cute and adorable when that little 10 pound puppy jumps up on you, your family members and your friends. Many people reward this behavior on the part of a small puppy with kisses and treats.

This is a huge mistake, however, since that cute little puppy may soon become a full grown dog who could weigh well in excess of 100 pounds. Suddenly that cute jumping behavior is no longer quite so cute.

In addition to being annoying, jumping up on people can be dangerous as well. A large, heavy dog, jumping enthusiastically, can easily knock over a child or an older or handicapped adult. In today's litigious society, such an incident could easily make you, as the dog's owner, the subject of an unwanted lawsuit.

The time to teach a dog that jumping up on people is unacceptable is when he is still young and easy to handle. Retraining a dog that has been allowed to jump up on people can be difficult for the owner, and confusing for the dog.

When the puppy tries to jump on you or another member of your family, gently but firmly place the puppy's feet back on the floor. After the puppy is standing firmly on the floor, be sure to reward and praise him.

It is important for every member of the family, as well as frequently visiting friends, to understand this rule and follow it religiously. If one member of the family reprimands the dog for jumping and another praises him, the dog will be understandably confused. As with other dog training issues, consistency is the key to teaching the dog that jumping is always inappropriate.

When praising and rewarding the dog for staying down, it is important for the trainer to get down on the dog's level. Giving affection and praise at eye level with the puppy is a great way to reinforce the lesson.

Problem #2 – Pulling and tugging at the leash

Pulling on the leash is another problem trait that many puppies pick up. Unfortunately, this behavior is also one that is sometimes encouraged by well-meaning owners.

Playing games like tug of war with the leash, or even with a rope (that can look like the leash to the dog) can unwittingly encourage a problem behavior.

The use of a quality body harness can be a big help when training a puppy not to pull, or retraining a dog that has picked up the habit of pulling on the leash. Try training the puppy to accept the body harness the same way it accepts the regular buckle collar.

When walking with your puppy, try using a lure or toy to

encourage the dog to remain at your side. A training collar, when properly used, can also be a good training tool for a problem dog. When using a training collar or choke chain, however, it is very important to fit it correctly, and to use a size that is neither too big nor too small for your dog.

When walking with your puppy, it is important to keep the leash loose at all times. If the puppy begins to pull ahead, the handler should quickly change directions so that the puppy fast finds itself falling behind. It is important to reverse directions before the puppy has reached the end of the leash. The leash should stay loose except for the split second it takes the handler to reverse direction. It is important to use a quick tug, followed by an immediate slackening of the leash.

When training a puppy, it is important to never let the puppy pull you around. Training the puppy to walk properly while he or she is still small enough to handle is absolutely vital, especially when dealing with a large breed of dog. If your 150 pound Great Dane hasn't learned to walk properly while he or she is still a 20 pound puppy, chances are it never will.

It is important not to yank or pull on the puppy's neck when correcting him. A gentle, steady pressure will work much better than a hard yank. The best strategy is to use the least amount of pressure possible to achieve the desired result.

Problem #3 - Escaping and roaming the neighborhood

A responsible dog owner would never dream of allowing his or her dog to roam the neighborhood freely.

Allowing a dog to roam on its own is irresponsible, dangerous (to the dog and the neighborhood), and probably even illegal.

Most towns have ordinances which prohibit dogs from being allowed to roam around free, so you could be in legal trouble if your puppy is found wandering the neighborhood unattended.

Of course sometimes that wandering dog is not the owner's idea, and many dogs perform amazing feats of escape when left on their own. The temptations for unattended dogs are many, including passing bicycles, joggers, children, cats and other dogs. It is much easier to prevent escapes than to recapture a loose dog, so let's talk about some preventative measures every dog owner can take.

Removing the motivation to escape is a big part of the solution. A bored dog is much more likely to spend his day plotting the great escape. A dog that is surrounded by everything he or she needs, like lots of toys, a soft bed, and plenty of fresh clean, water, is more likely to spend his or her day contentedly sleeping or playing with toys until the owner returns.

In addition, a dog with lots of pent up, unused energy is likely to try to escape. Try incorporating several vigorous play sessions with your dog into your daily routine. Make one of those play sessions right before you leave. If your dog has a chance to work of his or her energy, chances are he or she will sleep or relax much of the day.

Of course dealing with the dog is only half the problem. It is also important to make the property as escape proof as possible, through proper fencing and other measures. For dogs that dig, it may be necessary to extend the fence underground by placing metal stakes in the ground every few feet. For dogs that jump, it may be necessary to make the fence higher. And if none of these measures work, it may be necessary to confine the dog to the house when you are not at home.

TRAINING FOR PROPER BEHAVIORS

Teaching a dog proper behavior is very important.

While playing and having fun with your dog is certainly important, it is also important to teach your canine companion just what is expected – which behaviors are acceptable and which behaviors are not acceptable.

Dogs learn quickly, and every interaction between human and dog is teaching the dog something. Making sure you are teaching the right lessons is up to you as the dog handler.

Proper training techniques are important for the protection of the dog as well as the protection of the family and the community at large. While dogs are loving, protecting members of the family in most cases, a poorly trained dog can be dangerous and destructive. Making sure your new addition is a pleasure to be around and not a menace is up to you as the owner.

As we have seen so far in this book, the relationship between humans and dogs goes back for many thousands of years, and dogs have been domesticated longer than any other animals.

This means that humans and dogs have developed a bond not shared by many other domesticated animals. And this strong bond is very useful when training any dog!

All potential dog owners and would be dog trainers should understand how dog society works in the absence of humans.

It is important to understand the pack hierarchy, and to use that hierarchy to your advantage as you train your dog.

All pack animals have a lead animal, and in the case of dogs it is the alpha dog. All other members of the pack look to the alpha dog for direction and guidance. The alpha dog in turn provides important leadership in hunting, fending off other predators, protecting territory and other vital survival skills. This pack arrangement is what has allowed wolves and wild dogs to be such successful predators, even as other large predators have been driven to extinction.

What all this means to you as the dog trainer is that you must set yourself up as the pack leader –the alpha dog if you will– in order to gain the respect and trust of your dog. If the dog does not recognize you as is superior and its leader, you will not get very far in your training program.

Respect is not something that can be forced. It is rather something that is earned through the interaction of human and dog.

As the dog learns to respect and trust you, you will begin to make great strides in your training program. A training program based on mutual respect and trust is much more likely to succeed in the long run than one that is based on fear and intimidation.

A fearful dog is likely to at one point become a biting dog, and that is definitely one thing you do not want in your life. Rewarding the dog when he does the right thing, instead of punishing him for doing the wrong thing, is vitally important to the success of any training program.

Punishment only confuses and further frightens the dog, and it can set a training program back weeks if not months. It is important to give the dog the option to do the right thing or the wrong then, and to reward the dog when it makes the right decision.

For instance, if the dog chases joggers, have a friend jog by while you hold the dog on the leash.

If the dog attempts to chase the "jogger", sit him back down and start again.

You are not punishing the wrong decision; you are simply providing the choice.

When the dog sit calmly by your side, give him a treat and lots of praise. The dog will quickly learn that sitting is the right choice and chasing the jogger is the wrong choice.

THE END

GRAPEVINE BOOKS

From The Same Author:

PACK LEADER TRAINING TRILOGY

BOOK 1
TRAIN DOGS THE PACK LEADER'S WAY

*

BOOK 2
DOG TRICKS THE PACK LEADER'S WAY

*

BOOK 3
PUPPY CARE THE PACK LEADER'S WAY

SEE IN AMAZON.COM

GRAPEVINE BOOKS

CPSIA information can be obtained
at www.ICGtesting.com
Printed in the USA
LVHW092141131019
634093LV00001B/124/P